THE MINI ROUGH GUIDE TO
CUBA

ROUGH
GUIDES

YOUR TAILOR-MADE TRIP
STARTS HERE

Tailor-made trips and unique adventures crafted by local experts

HOW ROUGHGUIDES.COM/TRIPS WORKS

STEP 1

Pick your dream destination, tell us what you want and submit an enquiry.

STEP 2

Fill in a short form to tell your local expert about your dream trip and preferences.

STEP 3

Our local expert will craft your tailor-made itinerary. You'll be able to tweak and refine it until you're completely satisfied.

STEP 4

Book online with ease, pack your bags and enjoy the trip! Our local expert will be on hand 24/7 while you're on the road.

PLAN AND BOOK YOUR TRIP AT
ROUGHGUIDES.COM/TRIPS

HOW TO DOWNLOAD YOUR FREE EBOOK

1. Visit **www.roughguides.com/ free-ebook** or scan the **QR code** opposite

2. Enter the code **cuba446**

3. Follow the simple step-by-step instructions

For troubleshooting contact: mail@roughguides.com

10 THINGS NOT TO MISS

A PERFECT DAY

8.00am

Breakfast. Fuel up for the day ahead with a good breakfast at *El Café* in Old Havana. Tuck into tropical fruits, such as mango, papaya or guava, sliced or juiced, followed by eggs and bread, and local honey or jam.

9.00am

Parque Central and Capitolio. Start your day at the centre around the Parque. Admire the magnificent Gran Teatro, the *Hotel Inglaterra* and the imposing Capitolio, now open to visitors. Pop into the Cuban section of the Museo Nacional Palacio de Bellas Artes to see the comprehensive collection of Cuban art.

11.00am

Cathedral. Visit the Cathedral, once home to Columbus' bones, on a magnificent colonial square with street entertainers and have coffee at the nearby atmospheric, aromatic *Café O'Reilly*.

11.30am

Plaza de Armas to Plaza Vieja. Walk to the Plaza de Armas, visit the Castillo de la Real Fuerza, the Museo de la Ciudad and stroll around the nearby second-hand book market. Head down Calle Oficios to Plaza San Francisco and on to the restored Plaza Vieja.

1.00pm

Lunch. Close to the southwestern corner of Plaza Vieja is café and bar *La Bohemia* with tables on the plaza or interior patio. It offers everything from coffees to beers and light bites, Italian pastries and Cuban food.

IN **HAVANA**

2.00pm

Bus tour. Return to the Parque Central to hop on the Habana Bus Tour, which runs all day. Travel from the Almacenes San José artisans' market on Avenue del Puerto to el Vedado, Plaza de la Revolución, Cementerio Colón and Miramar. Another route takes you out past the fortresses to Playas del Este. You can get off at any stop and rejoin another bus later.

5.00pm

The Malecón. From Parque Central stroll down Prado to the sea and wander west along the Malecón taking in the golden light, musicians, flaneurs and fishermen. At *Malecón 663* you can enjoy live music and drinks on the rooftop terrace.

8.00pm

Dinner. While in Centro Habana, you can get a memorable meal at one of several *paladares* (small, family-run restaurants), such as *La Guarida* (see page 107), advance booking essential. Service is leisurely, enabling you to linger until the nightlife gets going.

10.00pm

On the town. Get a taxi to el Vedado for a great evening of music, dance, art, theatre and fashion. Fábrica de Arte Cubano showcases the latest in Cuban talent in a converted oil factory. Have drinks first on the beautiful terrace of *El Cocinero* next door. Finish the night back in Centro at the wildly popular *El Bleco* bar facing the sea. For a quieter drink, stay in el Vedado and head to lovely, artsy *El Madrigal*.

CONTENTS

OVERVIEW

The largest island in the Caribbean, Cuba is blessed with pristine beaches, fascinating old cities with myriad architectural styles, Latin music all with hip-swivelling rhythms, a surfeit of rum and the world's finest hand-rolled cigars.

For much of the twentieth century, Cuba occupied a leading role on the world stage wholly disproportionate to its small size and lack of economic clout. From the overthrow of the dictator Fulgencio Batista at the end of 1958 to Fidel Castro's tenacious hold on power and declarations of socialism, this small Caribbean nation has assumed near-mythical status as a living laboratory of social experimentation, political defiance and a people's perseverance.

LEGACY OF THE REVOLUTION

For nearly half a century a combative Fidel Castro weathered the opposition of the US government and the hostility of Cuban exiles in Miami. His successor, his brother Raúl, continued his legacy with a few modifications (Raúl himself was succeeded as president by Miguel Díaz-Canel in 2018). Emerging private businesses were

THE FACE OF CUBA

Cuba's eleven million people have a distinctively mixed heritage that reflects the twists and turns of the island's history: Indigenous Taínos, enslaved Africans, Spaniards and French and Chinese labourers have all settled on the island. Across the centuries these ethnic communities have mixed, and today most Cubans are of mixed race.

permitted in late 2010 by Raúl with further opportunities (with caveats) granted in 2021. The Cuban people have been required to make repeated sacrifices in the face of the US trade embargo and the collapse of the Soviet Union with its support and trade. The pandemic weakened an already floundering economy and the unification of the island's two currencies in 2021 has done nothing to improve the outlook. Fuel

Cuban performance artists in colourful outfits

and food shortages persist. Many Cubans, mainly the youthful, have given up and voted with their feet: some half a million have gone into exile – to the States, Europe, and Central America since the pandemic.

As one of the last Communist hold-outs in the world, this nation is a true curiosity. With much of the rest of the planet racing ahead, Cuba moves along in slow-motion. Behemoth American cars from the 1940s and 1950s, patched and propped up, lumber down the streets of dimly lit cities. In rural areas cars give way to oxen-led carts, horse drawn carts, Chinese bicycles and pedicabs. Data on cell phones was permitted in 2018, but 25 percent of the nation are not connected to the internet.

CUBAN REALITY

Everything has always creaked and spluttered in hard-pressed Communist Cuba. The economy thrives or falters in line with

School children in Havana

world trends, hampered additionally by the US trade embargo and hurricane damage. Many families continue to live in overcrowded conditions in run-down housing, and the average wage for someone who works for the state is the equivalent of US$20 a month.

In the early 1990s Castro needed to reorganize the economy after the collapse of the Eastern Bloc which had formerly subsidized Cuba. In 1993 it became legal for Cubans to hold US currency. Much of the economy was given over to the dollar, with many products and foods available only in dollar stores. Those with access to US currency soon had the advantage, and a decade later there was a deepening split between the haves and have-nots. Castro was forced to take action to halt the division, declaring that all foreign currency had to be exchanged for *pesos convertibles*, with a steep tax on converting US dollars. In 2021, the peso convertible, CUC, was unified with the Cuban peso, CUP. Runaway inflation with thriving black markets has seized the island.

The glaring deficiencies of the Cuban economy and needs of the Cuban people are impossible to ignore. Cubans also enjoy no real freedom of speech or press. However, unprecedented protests against the government and shortages rocked the nation in 2021; further protests were staged in March 2024. In 2021, more than 1,600 protesters were arrested; many were sent to prison and more than six hundred are still detained. Still, one doesn't see the heart-wrenching poverty in Cuba common in other parts of Latin America. Housing is provided by the state and while Cubans don't get nearly enough with their ration books, they do have something to eat although food supply is not sufficient. All Cubans are entitled to free health care and education. Average life expectancy rose from 57 years in 1958 to 74 years in 2021.

Cuba's dilapidation, poverty and restrictions highlight the indomitable spirit of the Cuban people. And Cubans are as hospitable a people as you'll find, inviting visitors into their cramped homes given half a chance.

PARADISE ISLAND

In dire need of hard currency, Cuba has embraced tourism, which is now one of the country's top revenue earners. It's obvious why: for many Cuba is primarily an idyllic sun-and-sea bolt-hole. The white sandy beaches are dazzling, with the long shores of Varadero the best known. Amateur sailors appreciate the countless natural harbours, anglers search for marlin off the coast, while scuba divers explore coral reefs and sunken wrecks.

Most travellers opt for package tours, but Cuba's diversity tempts independent travellers away from the sea and sand. In the island's eastern corner is Cuba's highest mountain range, the Sierra Maestra, site of many uprisings; to the west, in Pinar del Río province, is the verdant Viñales Valley with its huge *mogotes*; and central Cuba has the lush Sierra del Escambray and the old sugarcane plantations.

Then there are the towns and cities. Havana combines fine Spanish colonial architecture, vibrant street life and a range of cultural opportunities; Trinidad, a gorgeous colonial-era gem; and Santiago de Cuba, a colourful Cuban cocktail of Spanish, French and African cultures.

HISTORY AND CULTURE

When Christopher Columbus disembarked on eastern Cuba on October 27, 1492, he penned a note exclaiming that the land was "the most lovely that eyes have ever seen". Indigenous groups including the Ciboney from Central and South America had lived on the island since at least 3500 BC.

In 1511 Diego Velázquez sailed from neighbouring Hispaniola with some three hundred conquistadors. Baracoa became the first of seven settlements across Cuba. Velázquez and his followers enslaved the native peoples and in the process exposed them to European diseases. Entire villages committed suicide, and by the mid-1500s the Indigenous population had declined from over 150,000 to just 3,000.

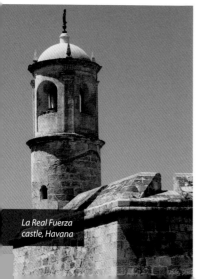

La Real Fuerza castle, Havana

PIRACY AND TRADE

Until the end of the sixteenth century, Cuba was a fairly insignificant Spanish colony. The port cities of Havana and Santiago de Cuba were heavily fortified to defend against pirate raids.

From the seventeenth century Havana became increasingly significant as a stopover point for treasure fleets. In 1762 British forces captured the city. They held it for only eleven months before returning it to Spain in exchange for Florida, but during this period trade was opened up to additional markets. A lucrative tobacco industry had taken hold in Cuba, and after 1763 the sugar industry skyrocketed. Though settlers brought the first enslaved Africans to Cuba in the early 1500s, hundreds of thousands were imported in the late eighteenth and early nineteenth centuries to meet the demands of the plantation industry.

Sugar island

By the middle of the nineteenth century, Cuba produced a third of the world's sugar and was considered one of the most valuable colonies in the world. Half a million enslaved Africans – nearly half the population – worked the plantations.

THE ROAD TO INDEPENDENCE

Spaniards born and raised in Cuba, known as *criollos* (creoles), managed the sugar-cane plantations but were excluded from the running of the country by Spain. During the nineteenth century some *criollos* (particularly in Oriente, the island's poorer, eastern region) became increasingly disenchanted and desired greater autonomy. On October 10, 1868 Carlos Manuel de Céspedes, a *criollo* plantation owner, issued a call for independence and liberated the slaves from his estate, La Demajagua. During the subsequent Ten Years' War (1868–78), fifty thousand Cubans – including Céspedes – and more than two hundred thousand Spanish lost their lives. Cuba remained a colony of Spain, but the war contributed to the abolition of slavery on the island in 1886 and cemented national consciousness.

In 1895 José Martí, Cuba's most venerated patriot, led the next and most important uprising against Spain. Born in 1853 and

José Martí statue in Havana

exiled at 18 for his political views, Martí became a journalist and poet. From exile in the United States he argued for Cuban independence. Martí was killed in an ambush during the War of Independence, which began in 1895 and in which some three hundred thousand Cubans lost their lives.

Throughout the nineteenth century, the United States, keenly interested in Cuba's strategic significance and its sugar market, had become increasingly involved in Cuban affairs. A US purchase of the island from Spain had long been on the agenda, even though Martí had warned of the dangers of becoming a satellite of the United States.

In February 1898 the USS *Maine* was sunk in Havana's harbour, killing 260 people. Although it was most likely caused by an accidental explosion, the United States used the sinking as a pretext to declare war. US victory in the Spanish–American War came swiftly, with Spain surrendering its claim to the island. A US provisional military government lasted until 1902, when Cuba became an independent republic. But the country was still subject to US military intervention which many claim crippled true independence.

FALSE INDEPENDENCE

For the next fifty years the United States, the largest importer of Cuban sugar, dominated the island's economy and largely controlled its political processes. The period was rife with political corruption, violence and terrorism. After 1933 Fulgencio Batista, though only a sergeant, controlled the strings of power through a series of puppet presidents before winning the presidency outright in 1940. He retired in 1944 but returned by staging a military coup in 1952. His dictatorship made it possible for him to invest some US$300 million abroad by 1959.

Since the 1920s disillusionment with the nascent republic – with its clear dependence on the United States and its lack of political probity or social equality – had grown steadily. Although Cuba had the second-highest per capita income in Latin America, prosperity did not filter down from the upper classes. In fact, the World Bank in 1950 declared as many as 60 percent of Cubans undernourished. In Havana there was a greater concentration of millionaires than anywhere else in Central or South America, and the capital was dubbed "an offshore Las Vegas" for its brothels, casinos and gangsters.

THE ROAD TO REVOLUTION

On July 26, 1953, rebels attacked the Moncada Barracks in Santiago de Cuba. The assault failed, but it thrust into the limelight its young leader, Fidel Castro. Castro was imprisoned and put on trial in a closed hearing; his legendary two-hour defence speech, later published as *History Will Absolve Me*, became a revolutionary manifesto. Castro was incarcerated on the Isle of Pines (now called the Isla de la Juventud) until May 1955, when Batista granted an amnesty to political prisoners.

Castro then fled to Mexico. The following year he returned to southeastern Cuba with a force of 81 guerrillas (including Che Guevara) crammed onto a small yacht, the *Granma*. Only fifteen reached the Sierra Maestra mountains safely. Incredibly, from such inauspicious beginnings the so-called "26 of July Movement" grew into a serious guerrilla army, aided in no small part by local peasants who were promised land reform.

CHE AND FIDEL: BROTHERS IN REVOLUTION

Ernesto "Che" Guevara (*che* meaning "mate" or "buddy" in Argentine slang) is the official poster boy and martyr of the Cuban Revolution, idolized by Cubans. His dramatic, beret-topped visage is seen on billboards and photographs throughout Cuba. Born in 1928 in Argentina, Guevara trained as a doctor before embarking on nomadic treks through South and Central America with a pile of Marxist literature in his rucksack. He met Castro in Mexico in 1955 and for the next ten years was Castro's right-hand man, as a guerrilla in the mountains then as director of the national bank (signing bills as, simply, "Che"), minister of industry, and minister of the economy. In 1965, he abandoned Cuba for new causes. He was killed trying to foment revolt in Bolivia in 1967.

Fidel Castro – for 49 years the president of Cuba, secretary-general of its Communist Party and commander-in-chief of its armed forces – was born in 1926 and trained as a lawyer at the University of Havana. The world's youngest leader in 1959, Castro defied all expectations to become one of the longest-serving heads of state on the planet. Fidel, as he is known to all, was a towering but frustrating patriarchal figure to Cubans. Yet he remained, above all, El Comandante.

Fidel Castro died on November 25, 2016 in Havana, aged 90. His ashes were transported in a funeral convoy from the capital to Santiago de Cuba, retracing the route of his victory march in 1959, as hundreds of thousands of Cubans, many wearing t-shirts with the slogan "Yo Soy Fidel" (I am Fidel), lined the streets to pay homage to their late leader.

Following a disastrous offensive by government troops on the rebels' mountain strongholds in 1958, and the capture of Santa Clara by Che Guevara and his men on December 30, on January 1, 1959 Batista fled the country. The *barbudos* (the bearded ones) triumphantly entered Santiago, then marched into Havana one week later.

Castro by Guayasamín

FIDEL'S CUBA

Castro's fledgling government immediately ordered rents reduced, new wage levels set, and estates limited in size to 402 hectares (993 acres). A nationalization programme followed, and the government expropriated factories, utilities and more land, including an estimated $8 billion of US assets. The foundations were set for near-universal state employment. At the same time, the government instituted programmes to eradicate illiteracy and provide free universal schooling and health care.

However, a centralized, all-powerful state didn't please all Cubans. The media were soon placed under state control, promised elections were never held and Committees for the Defence of the Revolution (CDRs) were established to keep tabs on dissenters. In the early years of the Revolution, tens of thousands of people suspected of being unsympathetic to its goals were detained, imprisoned or sent to labour camps, along with such other "undesirables" as homosexuals and priests.

Between 1959 and 1962 about two hundred thousand Cubans, primarily professionals and affluent landowners, fled the country. Expatriate Cubans settled in nearby Florida, establishing a colony that would steadily gain in political and economic power. Another two hundred thousand abandoned Cuba as part of the Freedom Flights Program between 1965 and 1973 and some 125,000 followed in 1980 when Castro lifted travel restrictions from the port of Mariel.

The US remained fundamentally opposed to Cuba's political evolution and sought to isolate Castro in Latin America. In 1961 CIA-trained Cuban exiles attempted to overthrow Castro's regime, resulting in the Bay of Pigs fiasco. Soon after, Castro declared himself a Marxist-Leninist. Castro had not displayed any Communist inclinations in the 1950s, and some suggest that US aggression pushed him to ingratiate himself with the powerful Soviet Union and its Eastern bloc of trading partners.

In 1962 Soviet President Nikita Khrushchev installed 42 medium-range nuclear missiles in Cuba. US President John F. Kennedy responded by staging a naval blockade and insisting

THE BAY OF PIGS INVASION

On April 17, 1961, a force of 1,297 Cuban exiles landed at Playa Girón. The Cubans were CIA-trained and came from US ships waiting offshore; US-piloted planes had bombed Cuban airfields days before. US participation was denied at every stage. Castro's twenty thousand troops, assisted by artillery and tanks, repelled the invasion within 65 hours. Some 1,180 exiles were captured and ransomed for US$53 million worth of food and medicine. The victory boosted Castro's domestic and international status. Soon after, he declared Cuba a socialist, one-party state.

the existing missiles be removed. After six days of eyeball-to-eyeball challenge (or the "Cuban Missile Crisis"), Khrushchev backed down in return for the withdrawal of US nuclear missiles from Turkey. The same year saw the imposition of a trade embargo by the US (which Cubans call the *bloqueo*), which still remains today.

The ubiquitous image of Che

THE SPECIAL PERIOD

Until the end of the 1980s, Soviet trade and subsidies were crucial factors in propping up Cuba's heavily centralized and often badly planned economy. But the subsequent dismantling of the Soviet Union left Cuba bereft of food, oil and hard currency. The government announced the start of a "Special Period" in 1990, introducing new austerity measures. Though rationing had existed since 1962, it was increased to cover many more basic items.

With its economy in disarray, the government introduced a limited number of capitalist measures while maintaining a firm political grip. Foreign investment, in the form of joint ventures in the fields of tourism and mineral and oil exploration, was keenly encouraged.

Further measures, such as the legalization of small enterprises in 1993 and the introduction of farmers' markets in 1994, improved the welfare of some Cubans. Life was still hard, however, and in August 1994, 35,000 Cubans fled to Florida on makeshift rafts.

A NEW ERA

Castro turned 80 in 2006, but had to hand power "temporarily" to his brother, Raúl, while he underwent surgery. Poor health would continue to prevent Fidel from playing any prominent role in the country's political life. In 2008 Raúl was chosen as president of the Council of State and the Council of Ministers, and in November 2016 Fidel, Cuba's revolutionary leader, died at the age of 90.

Raúl Castro's first measures were to lift a range of restrictions on consumer spending for those with access to foreign currency. Cubans could own mobile phones and home computers, rent cars and stay in tourist hotels on the beach.

Putting public finances in order is a high priority. Agriculture was decentralized, and farmers given greater autonomy as part of a drive for greater efficiency. The number of state employees was drastically cut, while permitted categories of self-employment widened. Reducing the rationing system was announced at the end of 2023 and in March 2024 fuel prices were raised 500 percent, and the cost of electricity climbed for large consumers.

The year 2014 saw a thaw in US-Cuba relations as US President Barack Obama and Raúl Castro began "normalising" relations. In 2017 President Donald Trump overturned some of Obama's plans and restricted US tourism to Cuba. Fifteen Cuban diplomats were expelled from the US in 2017 following allegations of sonic attacks on US embassy staff in Havana. Miguel Díaz-Canel, a staunch ally of Raúl Castro's, became Cuban president in 2018 and replaced Raúl as head of the party in 2021. In January 2021, Trump placed Cuba on a list of countries that sponsor terrorism, thus sanctioning Cuba and complicating its relationship with the world. President Joe Biden reversed some Trump Cuba policies – including those on remittances, flights to regional Cuba airports and consular services, but the threat of an unpredictable Trump in the White House again leaves Cuba's path looking far from certain.

IMPORTANT DATES

1492 Christopher Columbus lands in eastern Cuba.

1511 Diego Velázquez begins Spanish settlement.

1519 Havana, founded in 1515, moved to its present site.

1868–78 Ten Years' War for Cuban independence – victory for Spanish forces.

1886 End of slavery in Cuba.

1895 War of Independence begins; José Martí killed.

1898 Sinking of the USS *Maine*; US defeats Spain, which surrenders Cuba to the US.

1902 Formation of the Republic of Cuba.

1933–58 Fulgencio Batista holds power as president.

1953 Fidel Castro launches failed attack on the Moncada Barracks.

1956–9 Cuban Revolution. Castro seizes power (January 1, 1959).

1960 Castro's government nationalizes all US businesses in Cuba without compensation.

1961 CIA-trained Cuban exiles defeated at the Bay of Pigs.

1962 Cuban Missile Crisis.

1990 Russian trade and subsidies disappear; new austerity measures begin.

1994 Exodus of some 35,000 rafters to Florida; most are returned to Guantánamo Bay Naval Base.

2006 Fidel Castro undergoes surgery. Replaced temporarily by brother Raúl.

2008 Fidel Castro announces that he will not stand for president; Raúl Castro is elected.

2014 Presidents Castro and Obama trigger thaw of Cuban–US relations.

2015 US and Cuban embassies reopen.

2016 US President Obama visits Cuba. Fidel Castro dies.

2017 Trump presidency halts progress in improving relations.

2018 Miguel Díaz-Canel becomes president.

2021 Díaz-Canel replaces Raúl Castro as Communist Party leader. Unprecedented street protests against the government rock the island.

2021-24 A severe economic crisis grips Cuba.

A street in Santiago de Cuba

OUT AND ABOUT

To the surprise of many first-time visitors, Cuba is no speck in the Caribbean. Nicolás Guillén, the nation's finest poet, described the island as a "long green alligator". Long it certainly is, at 1,250km (776 miles) from snout to tail. Nearly the size of England in terms of area, Cuba is divided into fifteen provinces and incorporates some 450 offshore islands, known as cayos ("cays" or "keys").

Given its size, you would need at least a month to explore Cuba fully. Most people begin their journeys in the capital, Havana, before heading to the prized tobacco lands further west and doubling back across the plains of sugar cane and some of the country's finest colonial towns in central Cuba. The eastern region, known as Oriente, has soaring mountains and Cuba's second and most vibrant musical city, Santiago de Cuba.

Resort hotels hug quintessential Caribbean beaches (mostly to the north) and although many package tourists stick to the coast, every region has charming, engaging towns, beguiling visitors to explore further.

HAVANA (LA HABANA)

The island's capital, **Havana ❶ (La Habana)**, with little over two million inhabitants, is one of the most intoxicating cities in the world. Ever since its early maritime days and through the 1950s – when gangsters who ran prostitution and gambling rackets made Havana synonymous with decadence – it has always had a slightly louche, languorous allure. That nostalgic appeal is still evident.

Today Havana is a one-of-a-kind, fascinating study in decay and rebirth. Unrestrained ocean waves and salty sea spray have eroded elegant buildings and the seawall of the Malecón, the

Colonial buildings in Old Havana

sumptuous promenade and roadway that traces the edge of the sea. Throughout the city, crumbling houses three and four storeys tall, somehow still standing, line backstreets where children play stickball and adults survey the street from their balconies or doorways. In Old Havana, magnificently restored colonial palaces and stately Baroque churches and convents crowd cobblestone squares. Once the finest colonial city in the Americas, Havana's grandeur has not been destroyed even by decades of crisis and neglect. No less defiant than Fidel Castro was himself, beneath the rubble this city is a living, breathing, vital and sensual creature.

Havana sprawls over more than 700 sq km (270 sq miles) and is divided into many districts. Those of greatest interest are La Habana Vieja (Old Havana), Centro Habana (Central Havana), el Vedado and – to a lesser extent – Miramar. The latter two districts are twentieth-century residential and shopping *barrios* that extend west of the old city. While most areas within a neighbourhood can be covered comfortably on foot, passing from one to the other usually requires a taxi or *bicitaxi* (pedicab).

OLD HAVANA (LA HABANA VIEJA)

The oldest section of Havana is the city's most spectacular, even if restoration work and gleaming coats of pastel colonial colours are leaving parts of it with a slightly more sanitized feel than the weathered working-class neighbourhoods that extend along the water and inland. As the location of the city's greatest historical sites, **Old Havana** is where you'll want to spend most of your time.

First founded in 1515 on the south coast, Havana was moved to this site along a vast natural harbour in 1519. During the sixteenth century a fleet of galleons laden with treasures used the port as a pit stop on the way back to Spain from the New World. By the late sixteenth century, pirate attacks prompted the building of extensive city defences – colossal forts, a chain across the harbour mouth, and prominent city walls – making Havana the "Bulwark of the West Indies".

The wealthiest residents lived with their slaves in grand mansions constructed in the *mudéjar* style, a Christian-Muslim architectural tradition dating from the Spanish medieval period. Cool courtyards bathed in penumbral light sheltered from the sun and street noise behind massive doors, louvred shutters, carved iron window bars *(rejas)* and half-moon stained-glass windows *(mediopuntos)*.

The presence of such architectural wonders, no matter how dilapidated, led UNESCO to add Old Havana (along with the city's early fortifications) to its World Heritage

Find that street

Cuban addresses usually include the street followed by a number. Helpful hints are also given: "e/ …" ("between the streets …") or "esq. …" ("corner of …").

List in 1982. In the central quarter buildings have been or are being spruced up, mainly with funds raised by the City Historian's Office, once headed by Eusebio Leal Spengler. Once restored, the buildings are turned into hotels, museums and galleries, or become once more the splendid old shops they used to be. Many other buildings are propped up by wooden columns: their arcades, fluted pillars and mosaic tiles teetering on their last legs, awaiting their turn. At night, away from the main restaurant and bar areas, the darkness of the streets is punctuated only by the neon glow of television sets from tiny front rooms and the occasional headlights of gas-guzzling vintage Chevrolets and Plymouths, though much of the historical centre is now a pedestrian-only zone.

Havana's past lives on, evoked in part by legendary locations from the pages of popular novels and the lives of fiction writers. These include Graham Greene's **Hotel Sevilla** (Trocadero 55 e/ Prado and Zulueta) where "Our Man in Havana" went to meet his secret service contact, and Ernest Hemingway's favourite watering holes (*El Floridita* and *La Bodeguita del Medio*), as well as the **Hotel Ambos Mundos** (Obispo 153) where he penned much of *For Whom the Bell Tolls*.

Old Havana is best experienced on foot, but you can also pick up a *bicitaxi* for a tour around the district with stops for photos.

Plaza de la Catedral

Havana's sumptuous **Plaza de la Catedral Ⓐ**, the focus of La Habana Vieja life, could be a stage set. The glorious Baroque facade and asymmetrical belltowers of the late eighteenth-century **cathedral** are the square's top attraction. The church, begun by Jesuits in 1748, is a thing of beauty; one half expects its bells to erupt in triumphant song. Its interior is surprisingly plain, but it once held the remains of Christopher Columbus. Just south of the cathedral are superb colonial mansions with bright shutters and *mediopuntos*, and an attractive little cul-de-sac **(Callejón de Chorro)** where an Art Nouveau building houses the Experimental Workshop of Graphic Arts and cafés. You can watch artists at work and items are for sale.

Of particular interest in the Cathedral Square is the **Museo de Arte Colonial** (San Ignacio 61 e/ Empedrado y O'Reilly; charge; tel: 7801 7458) housed in a handsome palace dating from 1622. Its most important occupant, Lieutenant Colonel Don Luís Chacón, lived there from 1726. Its little-altered architectural features are complemented by a large collection of seventeenth- and eighteenth-century furniture and eighteenth- and nineteenth-century tableware, as well as a wonderful collection of historic fans. Sip coffee at nearby *Fonda Al Pirata* (San Ignacio 76 e/ O'Reilly y Callejón del Chorro).

The cathedral with its Baroque facade

Close to the cathedral, you'll find the atmospheric bar-restaurant **La Bodeguita del Medio ❸** (Empedrado 207 e/ Cuba y San Ignacio), which according to Hemingway served Havana's finest mojito back in the day. Like pilgrims to Ernest's drinking shrine, all tourists seem required to pay their respects here and pay for an overpriced mojito. Art exhibitions are held down the street at the **Centro de Arte Contemporáneo Wifredo Lam** (San Ignacio 22 esq. Empedrado; free; www.wlam.cult.cu), named after Cuba's most famous twentieth-century artist. Books, manuscripts and photographs of the country's best-known novelist are housed inside the **Fundación Alejo Carpentier** (Empedrado 215 e/ Cuba y San Ignacio; free; https://fundacioncarpentier.cult.cu).

Plaza de Armas

Plaza de Armas ❹, centred by a statue of the patriot Céspedes and ringed by shaded marble benches is Havana's oldest square. It dates to the city's founding in 1519.

On the square's eastern side a small neoclassical temple, **El Templete**, marks the spot where the first Catholic mass was celebrated in 1519. Next door is the handsome *Hotel Santa Isabel*. To the north, the squat moated **Castillo de la Real Fuerza** (Fort of the Royal Forces; charge; www.habananuestra.cu/index.html) is one of the oldest forts in the Americas, begun in 1558 with a fascinating shipwreck museum.

The battlements afford views over the harbour, and the bronze *La Giraldilla* weather vane on one of the towers – depicting a woman scanning the seas for her lost husband, an early Cuban governor – has been adopted as

A writer's tipples

"My mojitos at *La Bodeguita*, my daiquiris at *El Floridita*" – a personal declaration of drinks and where to have them, attributed to novelist Ernest Hemingway.

the symbol of the city and of Havana Club rum.

In 1791 the seat of government and the governors' (or captains generals') residence were transferred from the fort to the newly built Baroque **Palacio de los Capitanes Generales** on the square's western flank. A magnificent structure that was the presidential palace and then the municipal palace until Castro seized power, it now houses the **Museo de la Ciudad de la Habana** (Museum of the City of Havana; free; tel: 7869 7358).

Columbus statue inside the Museo de la Ciudad

Beyond the courtyard with a statue of Columbus lie splendid marbled and chandeliered rooms, some housing old cannonballs and coaches, others decked out with gilded furnishings. The most hallowed room commemorates Cuba's nineteenth-century independence wars, with the first Cuban flag and venerated personal objects from generals of the day. One block south is the secondhand book and curios market where traders pitch up on alternate days, i.e. don't say "I'll be back tomorrow" as someone else will be in their place that day (Baratillo e/Obispo y Justíz).

Calle Obispo

Running from Plaza de Armas to Parque Central, the pedestrianized **Calle Obispo D** is Old Havana's most important thoroughfare. Here you will find some smart shops catering to those with money to spend, and you can peer into the courtyards of Havana's

Shopping in Calle Obispo

oldest homes. Equally fascinating are the two parallel, partly residential streets – O'Reilly and Obrapía – where neoclassical and colonial buildings intermingle with decrepit tenements. Restored Old Havana now extends all the way to Plaza Vieja and along pretty much all of Calle Obispo.

At no. 155, Museo de la **Farmacia Taquechel** (e/ Mercaderes y San Ignacio) is a beautifully restored pharmacy dating back to 1896, with floor-to-ceiling mahogany shelves supporting a lovely collection of nineteenth-century porcelain jars containing herbal remedies and potions.

Close by, on the corner of Mercaderes and Obispo, is the refurbished 1920s-era **Hotel Ambos Mundos**; Hemingway lived on and off in room 511 for a couple of years during the 1930s. The room is kept as it was during his time here. Those not staying in the hotel can visit the room for a small fee, or go to the rooftop bar for cocktails and see the views over Old Havana.

Nearby are several museums worth visiting as much for the glorious colonial mansions that house them as for their contents. The striking lemon-yellow **Casa de la Obra Pía** (Obrapía 158 e/ Mercaderes and San Ignacio; charge; www.habanacultural.ohc.cu) is a seventeenth-century architectural wonder featuring a magnificent portal brought from Cádiz in 1686. There is a lovely courtyard and the rooms have been adapted to house a furniture museum.

The owner, a member of one of Cuba's most important families, sponsored five orphan girls each year – an *obra pía* (work of piety) that lends its name to both the house and its street. The massive mansion opposite, nearly as impressive, houses the **Casa de África** (Obrapía 157; free; www.habanacultural.ohc.cu), with drums, costumes, carved figures and furniture from some 26 African countries, as well as a collection of objects related to *Santería*, the syncretic Afro-Cuban religion (see page 33) and various items

SANTERÍA: THE CULT OF THE GODS

Santería ("saint worship") is a syncretic religion derived from the Yoruba people in Nigeria and developed in Cuba by enslaved Africans. Practitioners worship a complex pantheon of deities *(orishas)*, each with a specific character and a parallel Catholic saint – a guise that allowed slaves to disguise the religion from their hostile owners.

Initiates are chosen by a particular *orisha*, and they will wear the specific-coloured beads of that saint and maintain shrines in their homes. The saints are believed to exercise control over almost every aspect of a person's life, but to communicate with them on matters of great importance, believers need the assistance of a *babalao* (priest), who will throw shells and perform other rituals to learn of the saints' commands. Saints' days are celebrations featuring Afro-Cuban drumming and dancing.

Many Cubans have at one time practised the rituals of *Santería* – even Castro, allegedly. While difficult to quantify, its popularity appears to be increasing. In many parts of Cuba, one can see people wearing the coloured beads of their saint – red and white for Changó, the powerful god of war, and blue and white for Yemayá, the goddess of the sea – and others dressed all in white for initiation rites "to become sainted".

related to Cuban slavery, such as manacles and traps. Musical performances are held here on Saturdays.

Swing by nearby **La Marca**, a tattoo studio with an art gallery offering clothing, design pieces and concerts (Obrapía 108C e/ Oficios y Mercaderes; www.instagram.com/lamarcabodyarthavana). The underrated **Museo Nacional de la Cerámica Contemporánea Cubana** is a haven for Cuba's outstanding artists including Wifredo Lam and Amelia Peláez (Mercadres 27 esq. Amargura; charge; tel: 7801 1386).

The streets of Havana are a living museum of chrome-finned wondercars imported during Detroit's heyday. Several that once belonged to pivotal Cuban figures – such as a 1918 Ford truck used by Fidel's father and Camilo Cienfuegos' Oldsmobile – are lined up in the new **Museo del Automóvil "El Garaje" Ⓔ** (San Ignacio 305-309 e/ Amargura y Teniente Rey; charge; tel: 7801 8140).

Return along Calle Amargura to the splendidly restored **Plaza de San Francisco Ⓕ**, with the imposing eighteenth-century **Basílica Menor de San Francisco de Asís** (charge; http://habanacultural.ohc.cu). The convent contains a museum of religious treasures and a beautiful cloister. Concerts are frequently held here. Nearby, you'll find several impeccable colonial-era houses with brilliantly coloured facades and art galleries.

Plaza Vieja

Follow Calle Teniente Rey to the beautiful **Plaza Vieja Ⓖ** (Old Square), which was originally conceived in 1587 and received a massive facelift, with assistance from UNESCO. On the south side is a fine eighteenth-century palace, known as **La Casona**, and its balcony gives a lovely view of the plaza. On the southwestern corner is the **Cervecería Taberna de la Muralla**, a microbrewery with bar. Find welcome respite at *La Vitrola* (www.condedericlahostal.com/la-vitrola) and *Café Bohemia* (www.havanabohemia.com/cafe)

Plaza Vieja has been meticulously restored

on the square. In the northeastern corner, on the roof of a yellow-and-white wedding cake of a building, is the **Cámara Oscura** (tel: 7866 4461; temporarily closed), which gives up-close views of the city as well as wider vistas.

By the railway station, between Calles Picota and Egido, is **Casa Natal de José Martí** (Leonor Pérez 314; charge; www.facebook. com/mcasanataljosemartiohc), the modest birthplace of poet and statesman José Martí. The numerous personal effects on display here leave no doubt about the fact that Martí is Cuba's pre-eminent national hero. East of here is San Isidro. Once a *barrio* of brothels in the early 1900s, San Isidro's streets (and much of southern Old Havana) are now painted in colourful murals – some depicting coded messaging. The new art movement is anchored at **Galería Taller Gorría** (San Isidro 214 e/ Picota y Compostela; https://galeriatallergorria.com). Popular rooftop bar *Yarini*, above, draws drinkers and musicians on a regular basis.

The Capitolio Nacional

Capitolio

Calle Brasil (also called Teniente Rey) leads directly west from Plaza Vieja to the monumental **Capitolio** and was reopened in 2018 following an extensive eight-year renovation (charge, daily tours available; tel: 7860 8454). A replica of the American capitol in Washington, DC and completed in 1928, it reflects the period when Cuba was in the thrall of the United States. Its vast bronze doors pictorially chart the island's history. The immense main gallery inside – the Hall of the Lost Steps – houses the third largest interior statue in the world and has a replica diamond in the floor, beneath the dome, that marks the spot from which all distances in the country are measured.

Directly behind the Capitolio is the former **Fábrica de Tabacos Partagás** ❶ (Partagás Cigar Factory; Industria 520 e/ Dragones y Barcelona), renowned for churning out famously strong cigars since 1845. The building is closed and although you can still buy cigars in the small shop, they are no longer rolled here. The factory is now at San Carlos (e/ Peñalver y Sitios) in Centro Habana (charge, tours available; tel: 7873 6056). Real cigar smokers should resist the temptation to buy from the *jineteros* (hustlers) gathered outside. Bear in mind that **customs regulations** are tight: you're allowed to take home fifty official cigars; and twenty individual loose cigars without official receipt (see page 95).

North of the Capitolio, on Parque Central near the classic *Hotel Inglaterra*, stands the magnificent **Gran Teatro de la Habana Alicia Alonso** ❶, completed in 1837. The home of the Cuban National Ballet drips with ornate balustrades, shutters and sculpted columns. The cavernous interior is hardly less awesome; visit during performances or on a tour (charge; tel: 7861 7391).

Those with the Hemingway bug can visit **El Floridita** ❷ (www.floridita-cuba.com), at the intersection of Calles Obispo and Monserrate, one block east of Parque Central. The writer immortalized the swanky bar in *Islands in the Stream*. A bronze statue of Papa now leans against the bar, his photos adorn the walls and his favourite daiquiri is now referred to as the "Papa Hemingway", with double rum and no sugar (barmen claim he was diabetic). The place is a bit of a tourist trap, but still capable of evoking the kind of hedonistic refuge expat writers adored.

On the same side of the Parque Central is the Art Deco **Museo Nacional de Bellas Artes** (charge; www.bellasartes.co.cu). This building contains the **Arte Universal** ❸ collection, with Latin America's largest collection of antiquities, as well as works by Goya, Rubens and Velázquez, while a few blocks northeast on Trocadero is the **Arte Cubano** ❹ section, an excellent selection of works by Cuban artists such as Wifredo Lam, Carlos Enríquez Gómez and Eduardo Abela, housed in the 1954 Fine Arts Palace. Many of the paintings in the Museo Nacional de Bellas Artes were left behind by ruling-class families who fled Cuba in 1959.

Opposite the Arte Cubano collection, housed in the grand presidential palace used by presidents (and dictators) between 1920 and 1959, is the **Museo de la Revolución** ❺ (charge; tel: 7801 5598), one of Cuba's most interesting museums. Allow a couple of hours to see this exhaustive exhibition of the trajectory of the 1959 Cuban Revolution. Many of the worn exhibits feel like unashamed propaganda, but that's all part of the fascination. The most absorbing sections chart the struggle to power with count-less maps, evocative photos of both torture victims and triumphal scenes, and assorted personal memorabilia from passports and worn-out shoes to Kalashnikov rifles and bloodstained clothes.

In a square outside is *Granma*, the boat that carried Castro and his 81 rebels from Mexico to Cuba in 1956; it is now enclosed in glass, guarded by military police and surrounded by other revolutionary relics, such as a tractor converted into a tank and the delivery van used in the failed attack on the Presidential Palace in 1957.

The Prado

West of the intimate streets of Old Havana is a wide boulevard with grand palaces. The loveliest avenue, the **Paseo del Prado** Ⓞ (officially known as Paseo de Martí), runs from Parque Central to the sea and officially separates Old

Havana from Centro. It was built in the eighteenth century as a promenade outside the old city walls. Grand but run-down buildings, with fading flamingo-pink and lime-green facades, and ornate columns, flank a raised promenade of laurels, lamps and marble benches. In the nineteenth century, after the city walls collapsed, this was the most fashionable strolling ground for the city's wealthy. Now it serves as a minipark for *habaneros*, from musicians and roaming couples to children playing on skateboards and a weekend art market. Two new modern hotels dominate the seaside tip.

Havana's forts

Cuba's most impressive forts sit brooding over the capital's commercial harbour. Take a taxi through the road tunnel beneath the water to reach them. The older one, built at the end of the sixteenth century, is the **Castillo de los Tres Santos Reyes del Morro** , better known as "El Morro" (charge; tel: 7791 1098). The views of Havana over the defiant cannons are magical.

The vast **Fortaleza de San Carlos de la Cabaña** **Q**, known as "La Cabaña" (charge; tel: 7791 1098), running beside the harbour, was constructed in 1763 after the English capture of Havana in 1762. The largest fort ever built in the Americas, it is well-preserved, and the gardens and ramparts are romantically lit in the evening. A ceremony held at 9pm (El Cañonazo) re-enacts the firing of a cannon that marked the closing of the city gates (charge).

The Presidential Palace

Swimming off the rocks at the Malecón

CENTRO HAVANA AND EL VEDADO

The walls surrounding Old Havana were razed during the nineteenth century to allow the city to expand westwards. The long, curvaceous **Malecón** (breakwater), a six-lane highway and promenade alongside the city's north shore, links the districts of Centro and el Vedado. The victim of harmful salt spray, the seafront drive is undergoing patchy renovation. Havana's youth congregate along the Malecón on fine evenings, fishing, canoodling, drinking and swimming off the rocks.

Although most visitors will want to concentrate on historic Old Havana, the newer districts provide a fascinating view of the areas where most people live and work. The most interesting districts are Centro and el Vedado. The former is a congested, lower-middle-class *barrio* (neighbourhood) with few attractions, although a walk along its bustling streets can be an eye-opening experience. El Vedado is the city's principal residential zone – the epicentre of middle-class Havana – with parks, monuments, hotels, restaurants, theatres and the University of Havana. Once the stomping ground of the elite in the 1950s, the "suburb" of Miramar today is home to foreign companies investing in Cuba, a commercial area, and numerous diplomatic missions of foreign governments.

Centro

Centro Habana (Central Havana) is a ramshackle residential and commercial area. The city's main shopping street, pedestrianized **Calle San Rafael**, traverses it from the Parque Central westwards. Nearby is Havana's small **Chinatown**, at Calles Zanja and Rayo. A few Chinese restaurants selling Cuban-Oriental food are all that remain of what was once the largest Chinatown in Latin America in the 1950s. Look for street signs and remnants of Chinatown in the buildings and visit one of the city's best contemporary art galleries – Gallería Continua in the converted Golden Eagle cinema established in 2014 (www.galleria continua.com).

Eating out in Chinatown

The neighbourhood of **Cayo Hueso**, just behind the Malecón, is a rough-and-tumble *barrio* once populated by cigar-factory workers. Today the main reason to visit is to see **Callejón de Hamel R**, where the late artist Salvador González dedicated himself to preserving the area's

Afro-Cuban culture. The alley is a kaleidoscope of colour and sculpture. Come for the Afro-Cuban rumba on Sundays at noon.

El Vedado

El Vedado is a leafy residential area of mansions and villas, spacious and orderly in comparison with La Habana Vieja and Centro. It had its heyday in the 1940s and 1950s, when such gangsters as Meyer Lansky held sway in the *Nacional*, *Riviera* and *Capri* hotels. Stars like Frank Sinatra and Ginger Rogers performed, and American tourists emptied their wallets in glittering casinos.

The Revolution put the lid on the nightlife by banning gambling and deporting the Mafiosi. Today, new boutique hotels of international standard welcome travellers, and this is still the place to come for nightlife, theatre, restaurants and bars.

Business is centred on **La Rampa**, the name for Calle 23 from Calle L to the sea. Along Calle O is the iconic, historic **Hotel Nacional**, host to politicians and the glitterati in its twentieth-century heyday. Opposite the *Hotel Habana Libre* at Calle – the *Havana Hilton* in pre-revolutionary days – is the **Coppelia ice cream parlour $**. At this institution, locals queue for hours for the ice cream. *Coppelia* was instrumental in the award-winning Cuban film *Fresa y Chocolate* ("Strawberry and Chocolate"), a daring film when it came out in 1994 which dealt with freedoms, homosexuality and revolutionary fervour in contemporary Havana (its title is a wry reference to the lack of choices of ice cream flavours – indeed, of all things – in Cuba).

A short walk up the hill brings you to the University of Havana, founded in 1728, a quiet, attractive campus of neo-classical buildings and two museums.

Directly east on Calle San Miguel, 1159 between Calles Ronda and Mazón is the **Museo Napoleónico** (charge; www.facebook. com/museonapoleonico.ohc). The mansion holds not only Empire furniture but also a remarkable collection of Napoleonic memorabilia: portraits, busts and even his pistol, hat and a cast of his death mask from St Helena. The contents, which belonged to Julio Lobo, a nineteenth-century sugar baron, and the house were appropriated by the state in 1960.

Coppelia ice cream seller

In the same year, the government acquired the **Museo de Artes Decorativas** (Calle 17, 502 e/ D y E; charge; www.facebook.com/museodeartesdecorativas), when its aristocratic owner fled the island, leaving her collection of fine art hidden in the basement. Each room in this grand villa is furnished in a particular style: English Chippendale, Chinese, Baroque or Art Deco.

At Calle 11 e/ Paseo y A is the **Centro Fidel Castro Ruz** (free; www.centrofidel.cu) an entire city block renovated to create a museum and study centre in homage to Fidel. His life story and that of the Revolution are exhibited across the site.

Massive marble mausoleums line the principal avenues of the **Cementerio de Cristóbal Colón** ❶ (Columbus Cemetery, entrance on Zapata y 12; charge; tel: 7881 5515), which is a vast city of the dead established in the late nineteenth century. Cubans come here to pray and place flowers at the tomb of La Milagrosa ("The Miracle Worker"), who helps people in need. It is said that she was buried with her infant at her feet, but when their bodies were exhumed, the child was cradled in her arms. There are some beautiful tombs including the Art Deco Pieta by Cuban sculptor Rita Long and the domed mausoleum of Catalina Lasa embellished with Lalique glass.

Northwest at Calle 26, esq. Calle 11, is **Fábrica de Arte Cubano** Ⓤ (www.fabricadeartecubano.com), a popular venue for concerts, art exhibitions, film screenings and more that attracts crowds of habaneros as well as tourists.

Plaza de la Revolución

The **Plaza de la Revolución** Ⓥ is a vast, stark concourse where political rallies are held; otherwise it is usually empty. The square is dominated by high-rise ministry buildings, erected in the 1950s by Batista, and the **José Martí Memorial** – a giant, tapering obelisk that looks like a rocket launch pad – with a pensive marble statue of Cuba's greatest hero and a **museum** about his life (charge; tel: 7859 2347). The obelisk's lookout gives superb panoramic views. Adorning the Ministry of the Interior building opposite is a giant iron sculpture-mural of Che and on the Ministry of Communications is the outline of the face of rebel fighter Camilo Cienfuegos. Both are illuminated at night.

The iron sculpture of Che on Plaza de la Revolución

Miramar and beyond

To the west is the exclusive district of **Miramar**. The

villas of the pre-revolution-ary rich, expropriated by the state, have now been turned into apartments or offices, but embassies along Avenida 5 still imbue the area with a privileged feel.

> ### Casa de la Música
>
> The Casa de la Música in Miramar is one of the best shows in town. This is where Cubans come to dance their hearts out to salsa and other rhythms played by live bands. And visitors join in too.

At the corner of Calle 14, the revamped **Memorial de la Denuncia** (tel: 7203 0120) has some intriguing exhib-its relating to CIA espionage. It also documents dozens of the CIA's attempts to assassinate Fidel Castro. Don't miss the Russian Embassy, between Calles 62 and 66, which looks like a giant con-crete robot.

Also worth a visit is beautifully restored Casa de las Tejas Verdes (Green Roof Tiles House; Calle 2 no. 318 esq. 5ta Avenida; free tours by appointment) dating from 1926 and now housing a centre for promoting modern architecture and design.

In Jaimanitas, artist José Fuster has decorated the streets and homes of the neighbourhood in colourful mosaic work – a la Antoni Gaudí's famous work in Barcelona. It's an incredible sight, known locally as **Fusterlandia**. The artist's home is open to visits and there's a shop to buy his tile work (Calle 226 y Av 3ra-A).

HAVANA'S OUTSKIRTS

Havana's sprawling suburbs contain a couple of places associated with Ernest Hemingway that are magnets for those seeking to trace the author's life in Cuba. From 1939 to 1960 he lived on and off in the **Finca La Vigía**, now the **Museo de Ernest Hemingway** (closed when it rains; charge; www.hemingwayhavana.com/en). The house is 12.5km (7.7 miles) southeast of Havana in San

ERNIE AND GRAHAM: LITERARY FOOTPRINTS

Ernest Hemingway's literary and personal footprints are as deep in Cuba as they are in Spain, and they've become part of the tourist fabric in both places. Hemingway wrote two books based in Cuba, *The Old Man and The Sea* and *Islands in the Stream*, and in large part he wrote *For Whom the Bell Tolls* (about the Spanish Civil War) from his hotel room in Havana. He was an island resident for two decades. Pilgrims can trace his life in Cuba at various sites, including Finca La Vigía, Cojímar, *El Floridita*, *La Bodeguita del Medio* and the *Hotel Ambos Mundos*. Despite chummy photos with Castro (they met at the annual Hemingway Fishing Tournament, which Fidel won), the writer's views on the Revolution are elusive, although all Cubans accept him as a fervent supporter. His views notwithstanding, it is certain that he identified with the Cuban people. Hemingway abandoned Cuba in 1960 and committed suicide shortly thereafter in Idaho.

Graham Greene's classic novel about Cuban intrigue, *Our Man in Havana*, was first published in 1958. Not only is it an evocative portrait of sleazy 1950s Havana, with scenes set in the *Nacional* and *Sevilla* hotels and the *Tropicana* nightclub, it's also eerily prescient, as the hero invents drawings of Soviet weapons hidden in the Cuban countryside, just a few years before the USSR placed 158 missiles in Cuba. Greene was a great supporter of the Revolution, praising Castro, the war against illiteracy, the lack of racial segregation and the support of the arts. When he went to Cuba to do research for the book in 1958, he took supplies for Castro, who was secluded in the Sierra Maestra, in exchange for an interview that never took place. Greene's support wavered though when he learned of the Revolution's forced labour camps in the 1960s.

Francisco de Paula, so you will have to take a taxi. The mansion looks much as Hemingway left it but was meticulously renovated by a joint US-Cuban project to preserve the author's papers. Among the relics are nine thousand books, Hemingway's original Royal typewriter and innumerable bull-fighting posters and animal heads – mementoes from Spain and Africa. Visitors can only look in through the open doors and

A bust of Ernest Hemingway

windows, but you get an excellent view of the large, airy rooms and their contents.

Hemingway kept the *Pilar* 10km (6 miles) east of Havana at **Cojímar**. Next to the little fort is a Hemingway bust, looking out over the bay. His captain and cook aboard the *Pilar* was the fisherman Gregorio Fuentes. Until his death at the age of 104 in 2002, Gregorio would regale visitors with tales of his hero. He always denied that he was Santiago, the title character in *The Old Man and the Sea*, but he did not dispute that it was in Cojímar that Hemingway found the inspiration for his famous novel. The little fishing village is now unrecognizable from Hemingway's description.

Approximately 18km (11 miles) east of Havana (twenty minutes' drive), the long, beautiful sandy **Playas del Este** (Eastern Beaches) are a big draw. They are the closest beaches to the capital and particularly lively on Sundays.

WESTERN CUBA

Due west of Havana are **Artemisa and Pinar del Río provinces**, Cuba's westernmost region – a finger of land with the Gulf of Mexico to the north and the Caribbean to the south. It contains some of Cuba's most beautiful countryside among the lush Guaniguanico mountains and surrounding patchwork of verdant fields, where the world's finest tobacco is cultivated. In the beautiful UNESCO-protected Viñales Valley, tobacco fields *(vegas)*, royal palms and ancient limestone formations *(mogotes)* produce spectacular scenery. In this resolutely agricultural region, oxen pulling ploughs that till the red-earth fields and cowboy farmers *(guajiros)* on horseback are much more common than cars. Horse riding, walking, bicycling, excellent farm-to-fork fresh food, the somnolent pace and breathtaking countryside make it one of Cuba's certain highlights.

There are beaches and excellent diving further west, but for most visitors the star attractions are the irresistible little town of Viñales and its beautiful valley. Many visitors take organized daytrips to the region from Havana hotels, but an overnight stay in Viñales – overlooking the valley – is highly recommended.

Start your explorations by driving west to Artemisa on the *autopista* (highway) linking Havana with the city of Pinar del Río. About 63km (39 miles) along the highway, a turnoff leaves the level, palm-dotted plains for **Soroa ❷**, where the richly endowed national orchid garden nestles in the mountain foothills near a tourist complex. A guided tour reveals orchids in bloom, lychee and mango trees, coffee plants and splendid specimens of *jagüey* and *ceiba* trees. There is a *mirador* (lookout) and a waterfall, while the bar in the newly renovated Castillo de las Nubes complex also has stunning views over the mountains. Close to Soroa is the mountain eco-community of **Las Terrazas** (www.lasterrazas.cu)

Oxen ploughing the Viñales Valley

with a hotel, restaurants and guides for birdwatching, coffee plantation ruins and beautiful river pools.

PINAR DEL RÍO

At the end of the highway, 175km (109 miles) west of Havana, the small city of **Pinar del Río** ❸ has a busy commercial centre. Along the main street, Calle José Martí, low-rise neoclassical buildings in blues, yellows, greens and orange have a stately but dilapidated quality. You'll find a small, touristy tobacco factory, **Fábrica de Tabacos Francisco Donatien** (Maceo 157; charge; tel: 4877 3069), housed in an old jail near the Plaza de la Independencia.

The road southwest from the city to San Juan y Martínez leads deep into tobacco's heartland – the **Vuelta Abajo** – where the world's greatest tobacco is grown. Amid fields of big green leaves ripening in the sun and plantations covered in white gauze sheets stand steep-roofed barns where leaves are hung on poles with a needle and thread and then dried, turning them from green to brown.

If you continue to the western tip of the island you come to the **Península de Guanahacabibes ❹**, a Natural Biosphere Reserve covering 1,175 sq km (730 sq miles). At La Bajada (where there is an ecological station to hire guides) the road divides, heading west 52km (32 miles) to **Cabo de San Antonio** for sea pools, birds and American crocodiles. Alternatively, 12km (7 miles) south of La Bajada at **María la Gorda**, on the eastern shore of the **Bahía de Corrientes**, a solitary hotel offers good diving.

Some 27km (17 miles) to the north of Pinar del Río lies the most picturesque corner of Cuba. The deeply green **Viñales Valley** is spattered with *mogotes*, sheer-sided round-topped limestone masses covered in thick vegetation. These are the remnants of a collapsed cavern system that was created underwater at least 150 million years ago, in the Jurassic period. Tobacco (of slightly lesser quality than in the Vuelta Abajo) grows here in a patchwork of fields and dries in *secaderos (leaf-drying huts)*. Cigar-chomping *guajiros* in huge straw hats urge on their oxen, as vultures swoop overhead. At any time of day you can wander the fields and meet the farmers, who might even offer you a cigar.

VIÑALES

The little town of **Viñales ❺** is a pleasant, rural place, where colourfully painted, single-storey houses with porches line the straight streets.

Near the Cupet petrol station as you leave town heading north towards Puerto de Esperanza, there is a delightful **Jardín Botánico**. The garden was first planted in the 1930s and has been maintained by the same family ever since. A guide will show you around the fruit trees and flowers and let you taste the produce (tip expected).

Nearby a couple of local tourist sights, on all the package excursions, have curiosity value but not much else. One limestone *mogote* just west of town was painted by Leovigildo González Murillo in 1961 with a **Mural de la Prehistoria** (Mural of Prehistory) – commissioned by Castro himself – that is 120m (370ft) high and 160m (525ft) long. The garish painting, an exercise in bad judgement and sloppy execution, depicts evolution from an ammonite to a dinosaur to advanced "Socialist Man", *Homo sapiens*. All the creatures depicted were indigenous to the area. Eight kilometres (5 miles) to the north, the extensive **Cueva del Indio** (Indian Cave) was used as a refuge by Indigenous groups after the conquest. More interesting is the climb to **Gran Taverna de Santo Tomás**, the largest cave system in Cuba at 46 km long. A visit to a local goats' cheese farm, **El Olivo**, brings the promise of a platter of the award-winning delicious stuff.

ISLANDS NORTH & SOUTH

Just off the north and south coasts are four contrasting islands. Two hours from Viñales, and often visited on a day trip, are the lovely sands and gorgeous seas of **Cayo Jutías**. To the north, **Cayo Levisa** ⑥ is a small coral cay, about 3km (2 miles) long and just several hundred metres wide at most points, which has pristine beaches, clear waters and coral reefs. The island is

Viñales Valley and its mogotes

a half-hour ferry ride from Palma Rubia (ferries leave twice a day). There's a well-equipped diving centre, and overnight accommodation is available in the *Hotel Cayo Levisa* bungalow complex, which has a restaurant and a bar.

On the other side of Cuba, stretching eastwards from Pinar del Río's southern coast, is the Archipiélago de los Canarreos. There are two main islands. **Cayo Largo** ❼, 25km (16 miles) long and the most easterly of the archipelago, might be your Caribbean paradise – if all you're looking for is a dazzling white beach and clear blue seas. Other than the kilometres of beaches, there's not much else of consequence here except mangrove, scrub and half a dozen comfortable all-inclusive hotels with a full programme of entertainment and watersports. Turtles nest in the sand at one end of the island. At the other you can go sailing, diving and deep-sea

The Mural de la Prehistoria

fishing or take a boat trip to **Playa Sirena**, an incomparable strip of sand a ten-minute ride away, where lobster lunches are available.

Cayo Largo, with its captive tourist audience, is considerably more expensive than the mainland. Some package tourists spend the whole of their holiday on Cayo Largo.

By contrast, the **Isla de la Juventud** ❽ (Isle of Youth) sees few tourists except those at the rather isolated

Inside Cueva del Indio

Hotel El Colony (on the Siguanea Bay, half way along the island's western shore), who come exclusively for the diving off the island's southwestern tip. Cuba's largest offshore island, some 50km (31 miles) in diameter, the Isle of Youth is not its prettiest. It is said to have been the inspiration for Robert Louis Stevenson's *Treasure Island*; pirates once buried their booty here. The island received its jaunty name in the 1970s, when as many as 22,000 foreign students (mainly from politically sympathetic African countries) studied here in no fewer than sixty schools, now closed.

Visitors today come for the panopticon prison (see box) where Fidel and Raúl were incarcerated in 1953, a series of caves at **Punta del Este** where you can examine enigmatic symbols painted centuries ago by Indigenous peoples, and **Cocodrilo**, Cuba's most isolated village where there are a couple of B&Bs, a marine conservation project and access to the gorgeous **Punta Francés** beach and wildlife.

For more accessible entertainment, **Nueva Gerona**, the island's little capital, is moderately attractive, with striped awnings along its smart, pillared main street.

MATANZAS PROVINCE

Matanzas province east of Havana – largely flat sugar-cane country – was in the nineteenth century Cuba's most important cane-producing region. For today's visitors, however, the focus is on the beach resort of Varadero, Cuba's biggest package tourism draw, with opportunities for side trips to atmospheric, time-warped towns and to the swamplands of the south coast.

VARADERO

Varadero ❾ has enthusiastic proponents and equally passionate detractors among its visitors. A long peninsula with many dozens of low-rise hotels, restaurants, bars and stores stretching right to the tip (and more of each on the way), Varadero doesn't feel much like Cuba at all. It is a package tourist enclave, and plenty of visitors fly in and never venture further afield, so almost the only Cubans they will encounter are on the hotel staff. If you want to see and learn what makes Cuba a fascinating place, though, you'll need to leave for at least a couple of daytrips. This is easy to arrange on hotel-organized excursions or by booking a taxi at or around the hotels.

Presidio Modelo

Just east of Nueva Gerona is the fascinating Presidio Modelo (Model Prison). The dictator Machado built this copy of a US penitentiary in 1931. Castro and 26 of his rebels were sent here after the storming of the Moncada Barracks; their ward and Castro's solitary confinement cell have been restored.

Souvenir sellers at Varadero

For many visitors Varadero is heaven: a 21km (13-mile) long, virtually uninterrupted white-sand beach with shallow, turquoise, clean waters. Varadero isn't a recent development by a government desperate for hard currency; it was in the 1920s that Varadero first attracted millionaires, who built palatial holiday villas. They were led by Alfred Irenée Dupont who bought up most of the peninsula and used to vacation at the opulent **Mansión Xanadú**, which he had built in 1930 and which is now an exclusive six-room hotel, and club house of the eighteen-hole Xanadú golf course (www.cubavaraderogolfclub.com). Tourism proper began after World War II with the construction of hotels and casinos.

However, the beach, Varadero's best feature, can be problematic. Northern winds kick up with considerable frequency, and lifeguards put out the red flags to warn of the dangerous undertow. Occasionally there's a strong smell from the oil pumps on the resort's outskirts, and mosquitoes can be a real annoyance.

Moreover, the resort is spread out over 17km (11 miles), with no real centre, so you need transport to get around.

On the other hand, Varadero has many extremely comfortable hotels (most of them the results of international joint ventures), open bars and an excellent range of watersports. If you tire of the beach, there are craft markets in town and organized excursions to every conceivable point of interest on the island – including Havana.

Varadero occupies a long, thin insular spit of sand, with water on both sides and a bridge to the mainland. Between Calles 25 and 54 there's something of a local community of Cubans, with ancient Cadillacs parked outside rickety wooden bungalows. The liveliest area is around Calles 54 to 64, with a shopping mall, a host of restaurants and bars, and the **Retiro Josone**, a pretty park set around a palm-fringed boating lake. Spreading several kilometres further east are the newest hotel complexes.

MATANZAS AND CÁRDENAS

These quintessentially Cuban provincial towns are a world apart from Varadero. Their poorly stocked shops, dusty backstreets and primitive transport provide Varadero's package tourists with some insight into Cuban life before they're whisked back to their hotels.

Matanzas ⑩, 42km (26 miles) west of Varadero, is busy and historic. Lying alongside a deep bay, it came into its own during the nineteenth century as the country's sugar capital. On the leafy main square, Parque Libertad, the **Museo Farmacéutico** (charge; www.facebook.com/museofarmaceutico) is a wonderfully preserved French chemist's shop, founded in 1882. East towards the bay is the neo-classical **Catedral de San Carlos Borromeo** and the impressive buildings on Plaza de la Vigía: the **Palacio de Junco**, which houses a second-rate provincial museum; the restored 1863 **Teatro Sauto**, a lovely theatre with tiers of wrought-iron boxes, marble statues and a painted ceiling; the exquisite handmade books of **Ediciones Vigía**; and the sculpture-decorated San Juan River path. Visit the elevated **Ermita de Monserrate**, too, with its views over the city and Yumurí Valley, and you can also listen for live rumba in the streets

Las Cuevas de Bellamar, a short distance east, are Cuba's oldest tourist attraction. These caves were discovered by chance in 1861 by a Chinese workman. Tours (in English) take you down into a vast chamber for views of the many stalactites and stalagmites.

Fortunes have changed for the town of **Cárdenas ⓫**, 15km (9 miles) east of Varadero. Once the island's most important sugar-exporting port, it's now a somewhat ramshackle place. But the main square is elegant, and the **Museo Municipal Oscar María de Rojas** (Plaza Echeverría e/ Avenidas 4 y 6; charge; tel: 4552 2417),

On the street at Cárdenas

the second oldest museum in the country, houses a quirky collection of items. There is also the **Museo de la Batalla de Ideas** (Calle 12 y Plaza Echeverría; charge; tel: 4552 1056). Inaugurated by Castro in 2001, it documents the campaign for the repatriation of Elián, a local boy who was at the centre of international controversy in 1999–2000. His mother died while fleeing with him to Miami, but after months of heated controversy he was returned by the US authorities to Cuba to live with his father.

ZAPATA PENINSULA

The **Zapata Peninsula** is the largest wetland area in the Caribbean – it is flat as a pancake and covered in mangrove swamps and grassland plains. Its protected wildlife includes crocodiles, manatees and numerous species of birds. Frankly, though, you are

Cabaña on stilts at Guamá

unlikely to see any interesting wildlife unless you take a guided bird-watching trip from **Playa Larga**. You can see penned reptiles at the Cuban crocodile conservation centre at **La Boca**, a popular tourist site where you can learn about these endangered crocs.

Battle beach

A billboard at the Bag of Pigs reads: "Playa Girón: La Primera Derrota del Imperialismo en América Latina" (The First Defeat of Imperialism in Latin America).

A more appealing prospect is picturesque **Guamá** ⑫, which is about half an hour by boat from La Boca along an artificial channel and then across the vast **Laguna del Tesoro** (Treasure Lake). Legend has it that the Indigenous people dumped their jewels into the water rather than surrender them to Spanish *conquistadores*. Guamá is a group of tiny islands connected by wooden bridges. A few visitors stay in the thatched *cabañas*, but most people just come to wander along the boardwalk, greet the ducks and egrets, and have a meal.

It may be peaceful now, but the Zapata Peninsula is best known for the violence and bloodshed that once visited its shores. South of La Boca you soon come to Playa Girón – site of the 1961 US-led **Bay of Pigs** invasion (see page 20), in which more than a hundred people were killed. At irregular intervals along the often crab-Infested road are a number of concrete memorials to those who died during the invasion. You can stay at B&Bs on the sand at quiet and lovely Caletón, **Playa Larga**, or in B&Bs at the community of **Playa Girón** ⑬, where the already scruffy beach is further spoiled by a concrete breakwater. One major attraction, however, is the excellent **Museo Playa Girón** (charge; tel: 4598 4122) which serves as an emotional memorial to the three-day Bay of Pigs debacle.

Palacio de Valle

CENTRAL CUBA

Central Cuba is dominated by historic cities and beautiful beaches – especially on the north coast – Cayo Santa María, Cayo Coco and Guillermo, new resorts on Cayo Paredón Grande and Cayo Cruz, and Playa Santa Lucía. Few people explore central Cuba's hinterlands.

Central Cuba comprises five provinces: Cienfuegos, Villa Clara, Sancti Spíritus, Ciego de Àvila and Camagüey. Each focuses on a provincial city of the same or similar name, with the exception of Sancti Spíritus, home to the provincial city and gorgeous south coast Trinidad. The Sierra del Escambray dominate the southern area.

To the east of Sancti Spíritus, towns lie on flat plains. This used to be the main sugar cane growing area in the 1970s, but the collapse of the sugar-for-oil trade with the USSR in the 1990s led to the closure of many sugar factories. In Camagüey, the cattle-ranch province, watermills and *vaqueros* (cowboys) on horseback punctuate the skyline.

CIENFUEGOS

The best feature of the port city of **Cienfuegos** ⓮ (250km/155 miles southeast of Havana), the only city in Cuba founded by the French, is its position, set at the back of a large bay. Despite the industry on its periphery, the centre is attractive, with pastel-coloured neoclassical buildings. Described as the "Pearl of the South", it now has UNESCO World Heritage Site status.

The focal point in town is **Parque José Martí**, one of the grandest squares in the country. Here you will find most of the major historical buildings, where the city was founded in 1819. The influence of nineteenth-century French immigrants can be seen in the architecture, although there are several styles, including neoclassical and Art Deco. Take a guided tour of the town's finest colonial building, the **Teatro Tomás Terry**, on the north side of the square. Built in 1890, it was named after a rich sugar plantation owner, once a poor émigré from Venezuela. The interior, largely original, has a lovely frescoed ceiling and a semi-circle of tiered boxes and wooden seats. Enrico Caruso and Sara Bernhardt once performed here; check the box office for performance

Botanical highlight

The Jardín Botánico Soledad (charge; tel: 4354 5115), 23km (14 miles) outside Cienfuegos at Pepito Tey on the road to Trinidad, is the oldest botanical garden in Cuba (it dates from 1899) and one of the best tropical gardens in the world. Tour operators in Cienfuegos can arrange guided tours; alternatively, go straight there and join a tour at the entrance.

information. The **Catedral de la Purísima Concepción**, built in 1870, is on the east side of the square. It has two bell towers and an attractive interior with stained-glass windows depicting the twelve apostles.

The Paseo del Prado is the town's principal thoroughfare and the longest boulevard in Cuba, a portal-lined road that takes you down to the spit of land protruding into the bay past waterside villas. At the edge of Punta Gorda, near the end of the Malecón (Calle 37), is the spectacular **Palacio del Valle**. This kitsch, Moorish Revival-style mansion (with a few other styles mixed in), was finished in 1917. It is now a restaurant with a rooftop bar and is attached to the *Hotel Jagua* alongside.

At the mouth of the bay, on the western side, the **Castillo de Jagua** (charge) was constructed by the Spanish in 1733–45 (long before the city's founding in 1819) to ward off pirates. You reach the castle on a ferry from a terminal just south of the Parque Martí (Avenida 46 e/ Calles 23 y 25).

TRINIDAD

The scenic, undulating 80km (50-mile) road east from Cienfuegos to Trinidad skirts the foothills of the Sierra del Escambray, Cuba's second-highest mountain range. The beguiling town of **Trinidad** ⑮, the third of Diego Velázquez's original seven settlements, subsequently became rich through the smuggling, slave and sugar trades. Its sizable old town is endowed with marvellous Spanish colonial architecture and has been named by UNESCO as a World Heritage Site. Cuba could package it as a time capsule: it is the island's prettiest town and one of the finest preserved colonial cities in all the Americas. Even the cobblestone streets still remain in the old centre, which restrict traffic and make things difficult for bicycles and horses. There's been a preservation order on Trinidad since the 1950s.

The old town in Trinidad

Within easy striking distance of Trinidad are enough attractions to make a longer stay especially rewarding, including the fine beach of Playa Ancón, the lush Valle de los Ingenios (Valley of the Sugar Mills) and waterfalls and treks in the Escambray mountains.

Restored mansions of the well-to-do have been turned into museums, while art galleries, craft shops, artisan projects and restaurants occupy additional lovely old buildings. The city is known for its live music venues in the centre, several of which are open air or in covered courtyards of old buildings. However, entertainment is low key, and it's still a pleasant, relaxed place.

The old town clusters around the **Plaza Mayor**, a delightful square of painted railings, fanciful urns, greyhound statues and colonial buildings. The relatively plain church, Iglesia Parroquial de la Santísima Trinidad, is the largest in Cuba, with five aisles instead of three and hand-carved gothic altars. Beside it is the **Museo Romántico** (charge; tel: 5219 0250) with a collection of

School children make their way home

fine furniture and porcelain. The square's two other museums both have attractive courtyards and cool interiors: the **Museo de Arqueología Guamuhaya** (charge; tel: 4199 3420) in a beautiful mansion on the west side of the square traces pre- and post-Columbian history; the **Museo de Arquitectura Colonial** (charge; tel: 4199 3208) on the east side has examples of woodwork, ironwork, stained glass and other items culled from colonial houses; and a block to the north of the Plaza Mayor in a former convent is the **Museo Nacional de Lucha Contra Bandidos** (National Museum of the Struggle Against Counter-Revolutionaries; charge; tel: 4199 4121), which documents the campaign to weed out rebels who hid in the Escambray mountains in the 1960s. The 360-degree view from the yellow belltower is the big draw.

A block south of Plaza Mayor on Calle Simón Bolívar stands the grand Palacio Cantero, built in 1830. Painted pillars, scrolls, shells, pediments and drapes embellish the interior, eclipsing the historical artefacts and old furniture that now form the **Museo Municipal de Historia** (charge; tel: 4199 4460). It has its own fine tower, though climbing its rickety narrow stairs can be a trial.

Alongside, sellers of handmade lace and other crafts sell their wares (the needlework of Trinidad earned the city UNESCO Creative City status). Further afield, along Calle Sta Ana, you'll find the evocative ruins of **Iglesia de Santa Ana**, and overlooking the town from the north is the **Ermita La Popa**, a bricked-up church now partially incorporated into a new hotel.

Aimless wandering is especially fruitful in Trinidad – and, since dozens of street names have changed and neither maps nor residents seem sure of what to call many of them, roaming without a plan is the only practical solution. Virtually every street has its own colonial treasure and feast for the eyes.

AROUND TRINIDAD

Trinidad's prosperity in the nineteenth century came from the fruits of 56 sugar mills nearby in the scenic **Valle de los Ingenios** ⑯ (Valley of the Sugar Mills). A *mirador* (lookout) with spectacular views is just 5km (3 miles) out of town. About 10km (6 miles) further east is Manaca-Iznaga, where you can explore a lovely colonial hacienda house and its startling, rocket-shaped *Torre de Manaca-Iznaga*. From the top of the tower, the Iznaga family would keep watch over their slaves toiling in the fields. Other plantation haciendas have been meticulously restored – notably Buenavista (with Italian frescoes) and San Isidro de los Destiladeros (with a new museum). Tours are available with the tour operators in Trinidad, or you could arrange a taxi tour. A steam train once used in the sugar industry traverses the whole valley for tourists occasionally. Ask at tour agency offices in town.

Playa Ancón ⑰, approximately 12km (7.5 miles) from Trinidad has an excellent strip of white sand and clear waters. Here you'll find diving at an offshore coral reef, a good choice of watersports and a scattering of hotels whose bars and sunbeds are available to all. Sun worshippers tend to congregate here, where there is a car park which serves as a transport hub for a tourist bus service and taxis or you can rent bicycles in town. North is Playa María Aguilar, site of a new luxury hotel, plus a string of beaches with snack bars and sun loungers stretching up to the attractive fishing village of La Boca (with restaurants and B&Bs).

SIERRA DEL ESCAMBRAY

More compact than the island's eastern and western ranges, the **Sierra del Escambray** (Escambray mountains), coated in luxuriant vegetation, are arguably Cuba's most beautiful range and easily accessible. Blessed with their own microclimate, the mountains are a wonderfully cool refuge from the heat of Trinidad.

To get to the **Topes de Collantes** ⑱ national park, take the road west of Trinidad for the steep 15km (9-mile) climb through dense forests of palms, eucalyptus and pines. You'll pass a health resort, a Stalinesque complex that has decent facilities but lacks life. Two excellent hiking trails conclude with beautiful waterfalls: Salto de Caburní, at 62m (203ft), and Salto Vega Grande. Wear sturdy shoes, as each hike is a steep trek of 4km (2.5 miles) along a narrow and often muddy trail. You can swim in the chilly natural pools underneath the falls. Jeep excursions can be hired at any tour agency in Trinidad. There's a national park charge (price dependant on the trail you intend to follow).

SANCTI SPÍRITUS

Approximately 80km (50 miles) east of Trinidad is **Sancti Spíritus** ⑲, one of Diego Velázquez's seven original townships. Although no match for Trinidad, it has some attractive colonial buildings. The **Iglesia Parroquial Mayor del Espíritu Santo** has foundations

Cayo Guillermo

from 1522, making it the country's oldest (though the present stone church was built in 1680). Nearby is the **Puente Yayabo**, the only remaining colonial stone arched bridge in Cuba.

SANTA CLARA

A must on the itinerary of all fans of the Revolution, **Santa Clara** ⑳ is a pleasant university city famous as the last resting place of guerrilla hero, Che Guevara. It was the site of the last battle, which started on December 28, 1958 and finished when news arrived that Batista had fled the country on January 1, 1959. An armoured troop train was heading from Havana to Santiago, but Che and his men ambushed it at Santa Clara. Four of the carriages are preserved at the **Monumento a la Toma del Tren Blindado** (Calle Independencia; free; tel: 4220 2758). You can go into the carriages and see some of the items carried on the train, as well as photos. At the **Plaza de la Revolución Ernesto Guevara** is a huge statue of

Che in battle dress, while underneath is the **Mausoleum** (free; tel: 4220 5668) where Che and his comrades who fell in battle in Bolivia in 1967 were interred when their remains were brought back in 1997. Next to it is the **Museo Histórico de la Revolución**, which has displays detailing Che's life and his role in the Revolution. The city has a flourishing LGBTQ+ scene focused on the El Mejunje cultural venue.

THE GARDENS OF THE KING

These offshore cays are reached by a causeway across the Bahía de Perros (28km/17 miles) and a further one east crossing the water north of Playa Jiguey.

Cayo Coco ㉑ is named not for coconuts but for a bird: the ibis, as revealed in Hemingway's *Islands in the Stream*. Ibises and other wading birds, often pink flamingos, can be seen balancing in the brackish waters around the principal causeway and a smaller causeway connecting the cay to **Cayo Guillermo**. In recent years, Cayo Paredón Grande and Cayo Cruz, further east, have been developed.

It's the impossibly white sandy beaches, the intensely blue waters, the excellent fishing and the kite surfing that draw holidaymakers. Large, luxury, all-inclusive resorts line idyllic Cayo Coco and Guillermo whereas the other cays have just a cluster of new hotels. A wide range of non-motorized watersports are available to hotel guests. If you hire a moped from your hotel, there are virgin beaches still to discover.

CAMAGÜEY

About 550km (342 miles) southeast of Havana, **Camagüey** ㉒ is an attractive colonial city – Cuba's third largest. Having been razed by Henry Morgan in 1668, it was rebuilt, with its narrow, twisting streets radiating haphazardly from the Hatibonico River as if to deter further pirate invasions. There are some half-dozen squares dotted around, each with an old church. Some, like Nuestra Señora del Carmen and Iglesia San Juan de Dios, have been nicely restored. The province's cattle-grazed plains hold little water, so the citizens fashioned huge earthenware pots to catch rainwater. Called *tinajones*, these still adorn many squares.

The city's most famous son, Ignacio Agramonte (1841–73), a general killed in battle in the Ten Years' War, was born here and his birthplace on Plaza de los Trabajadores is now a museum: **Museo Casa Natal de Ignacio Agramonte** (Avenida Agramonte 459; charge; tel: 3229 7116), a handsome, early nineteenth-century mansion. **Nuestra Señora de la Merced** church opposite has benefited from thoughtful restoration: the decorated ceiling is particularly striking.

Catching up with the news in Plaza del Carmen, Camagüey

A dashing equine statue of Agramonte forms the centrepiece of **Parque Agramonte**, just to the south. The cathedral occupies one side of the park, and the Casa de la Trova, around a floral patio, has musical performances afternoon and evening.

A ten-minute walk west down Calle Cristo brings you to a dignified eighteenth-century church, **Santo Cristo del Buen Viaje**. Behind the church is a great sea of crosses and marble saints in a picturesque cemetery. A few blocks north is the triangular-shaped **Plaza del Carmen**, which has been beautifully restored and is notable for the life-size statues of local people passing the time of day – some seated on sculpted chairs, reading newspapers, or in conversation with one another – by sculptor Martha Jiménez, whose studio is on the square. In one corner stands the **Convento de Nuestra Señora del Carmen**; dating from the early nineteenth century, the restored church facade is one of the most beautiful in Cuba and is unique in Camagüey for having two towers.

Another splendid feature of Camagüey – and marvellously restored – is **Plaza San Juan de Dios**, an angular old cobblestoned square surrounded by brightly hued single-storey buildings dating from the eighteenth century, plus a lovely yellow church with a fine mahogany ceiling and altar, alongside a restored former hospital. It's one of Cuba's prettiest plazas. Find plenty of open artists' studios in and around the square.

PLAYA SANTA LUCÍA

An hour-and-a-half drive (110km/68 miles) from Camagüey on the north coast, remote **Playa Santa Lucía** ❷ beckons sun worshippers with mid-range resort hotels and a handful of B&Bs strung along a particularly fine peninsular strip of sand. Each hotel backs directly onto the beach. A superb coral reef lies offshore, and diving here is excellent. Aside from a couple of roadside bars, however, nightlife is limited to hotel entertainment.

Horse and cart head to **Playa Los Cocos**, some 5km (3 miles) away; with sheltered aquamarine waters, it's a strong contender for the title of Cuba's most beautiful beach. Adjacent is La Boca, a very small community of waterside shacks with fish restaurants. Many visitors come to Playa Santa Lucía to dive with bull sharks in the channel between the village of La Boca and Cayo Sabinal.

EL ORIENTE: THE EAST

Prior to the Revolution, the east of Cuba was a single province known simply as el **Oriente** ("East"), and most Cubans still refer to the region with this name. El Oriente incorporates the post-revolutionary provinces of Holguín, Granma, Santiago de Cuba and Guantánamo. The stunning landscapes vary from the north coast's blue seas, coral reefs and exuberant banana and coconut groves clustered round thatched huts, little changed from earlier

Indigenous peoples' *bohíos*, to the towering peaks of the Sierra Maestra mountains, revolution sites, and limestone platforms and to the lush rainforest, waterfalls, archaeological sites and coconut-infused cuisine on the east coast.

The wars of independence began in Oriente in the 1860s, and nearly a century later Castro concentrated his power base in the inaccessible Sierra Maestra. There are stirring monuments and museums recalling these periods in Santiago de Cuba, the latter dubbed a "heroic city" or its many historic patriots.

The further east you travel in Cuba the more Caribbean it feels. Santiago de Cuba is renowned for its contributions to Cuban musical culture; the Oriente is the heartland of son, the traditional rural music that formed the roots of salsa, and many of the genre's greats (Trío Matamoros, La Vieja Trova Santiaguera and Elíades Ochoa, among others) got their start in Santiago.

HOLGUÍN PROVINCE

The province of Holguín begins bleakly around the busy capital but improves considerably as you travel north, where the countryside is lusher. **Guardalavaca 24**, 60km (37 miles) from Holguín, is an attractive resort, ringed by banana plantations. Watersports are excellent here and at the equally picturesque – but isolated – **Playa Esmeralda**, 2km (1 mile) west. All-inclusive hotels are dotted along the coast to the west, occupying horseshoe bays and sandy beaches such as Playa Pesquero Viejo and Playa Pesquero Nuevo.

There are plenty of possibilities for excursions in the vicinity of Guardalavaca. You can take a boat trip into the middle of Bahía de Naranjo to a simple aquarium, or arrange sailing and fishing trips from the marina. To the west is **Bahía de Bariay**, which has a monument claiming Columbus's landing (a fact contested chiefly by Baracoa, further east). Beyond the bay is **Gibara 25** (27km/17 miles north of Holguín), a captivating if sleepy little port town, known for its annual festival for films (https://ficgibara.icaic.cu).

About 6km (4 miles) south of Guardalavaca, on a hill amid a forest of palms and thatched homesteads, is **Chorro de Maita**  ㉖ (charge), the Caribbean's most important excavated pre-Columbian Indigenous burial ground. Fifty-six of the 108 skeletons found are on display. They date from 1490 to 1540 and lie exactly as they were found. All but one are Indigenous, buried in the Central American style with arms folded across stomachs. The one Spaniard lies in a Christian fashion with arms crossed on his chest.

Making music in Santiago

Banana groves coat the hillsides along the scenic 30km (19-mile) route south to **Banes** ㉗, a town of wooden houses with corrugated roofs. Castro was married at the church here in 1948, and the town's interesting **Museo Indo-Cubano Bani** (charge; tel: 2480 2487) has some fascinating finds from the area.

SANTIAGO DE CUBA

Many visitors prefer Cuba's second city (population 441,000) to the capital. **Santiago de Cuba** ㉘ (880km/546 miles southeast of Havana) is one of the oldest cities, with a wealth of colonial buildings. Unfailingly vibrant and seductive, it exudes a feel all its own. Enclosed by the Sierra Maestra mountains, Santiago can also be wickedly hot. *Santiagueros* negotiate their hilly streets by keeping to the shady sides, and they relax on overhanging balconies.

Santiago is Cuba's melting pot, with a friendly population of predominantly mixed-race residents: descendants of Spanish, French from Haiti, Jamaicans and huge numbers of enslaved Africans. Afro-Cuban traditions remain strong, reflected in *Carnaval*, which is still Cuba's best, and in music (walk down any street and a cacophony of sounds will emanate everywhere).

Founded in 1514, Santiago was the island's capital until 1553. It is regarded as a "heroic city" *(ciudad héroe)*, and locals are proud of the city's rebellious past. Seminal events brought it centre-stage again during the 1950s, when it assumed a major role in the revolutionary struggle. The attack on Batista's forces at the Moncada Barracks in 1953 thrust Fidel Castro into the national limelight, and it was in Santiago's main square that he first declared victory on January 1, 1959.

The city was badly damaged by Hurricane Sandy in 2012, losing most of its trees as well as many buildings, but subsequent repairs and a facelift to celebrate its 500th anniversary in 2015 mean the centre is now smart and attractive again.

Santiago historic centre

The most atmospheric part of the city is **historic Santiago**. Castro delivered his victory speech in the heart of the old town, from the balcony of city hall on **Parque Céspedes**. The attractive square is a genteel place with trees, gas lanterns and iron benches. Old Santiago's grid of streets unfolds here, a few blocks inland from the heavily industrialized harbour. Parque Céspedes is dominated by its twin-towered **cathedral**. A basilica was built on this spot in 1528, but what you see was rebuilt in the early nineteenth century after a series of earthquakes and fires.

On the west side of the plaza is **Casa de Diego Velázquez** (charge; tel: 2265 2652). Noticeable for its black-slatted balconies, it

Vintage car on a Santiago back street

was built in 1516 as the residence of the founder of Cuba's original seven *villas* (towns). The oldest house in Cuba and one of the oldest in the Americas, it is in remarkable condition. Housing the **Museo de Ambiente Histórico Cubano**, its rooms overflow with period furniture and carved woodwork and encircle two lovely courtyards. Across the square is the elegant *Hotel Casa Granda*, which opened in 1914 and hosted many celebrity guests and gangsters before the Revolution. Its terrace bar on the fifth floor affords excellent views of the cathedral towers and the city beyond.

East from the square, **Calle Heredia** is the epicentre of Santiago culture and tourism. The city's famous **Casa de la Trova** (music hall), which has hosted nearly all legendary Cuban musicians, is the centrepiece of both. Starting in midmorning, a succession of groups perform every style of Cuban music here, from *son* and *guarachas* to *boleros* and *salsa*. The intimate open-air space inside is the place to be in the evenings; at night the main groups play

Museo de Ambiente Histórico Cubano

upstairs. Calle Heredia is lined by day with artisans and souvenir sellers.

Down the street is the **Museo El Carnaval** (charge; tel: 2262 6955), a museum containing instruments, photos and artefacts from Santiago's carnival. It also occasionally hosts Afro-Cuban music and dance, as does the Artex patio up the street. Also on Calle Heredia is the **Casa Natal de José María Heredia** (charge; tel: 2262 5350), the birthplace of the early nineteenth-century Cuban poet and a cultural centre and museum.

Nearby, on Calle Pío Rosado, the **Museo Provincial Emilio Bacardí** (charge; tel: 2265 4501) has an excellent collection of artefacts detailing the history of Santiago, many items from the wars of independence and an archaeological hall that features a 3,000-year-old Egyptian mummy, two Peruvian skeletons and a shrunken head. The museum, in a grandiose neoclassical build-ing on a beguiling little street, is named for its benefactor and the town's former mayor, whose family founded the Bacardi rum empire.

One of Santiago's most delightful people-watching spots is **Plaza Dolores**, a shady plaza lined with colonial-era homes (sev-eral now house tourist restaurants). Pedestrianized **Avenida José A. Saco** (known as **Enramadas**) is Santiago's main shopping thor-oughfare. Its faded 1950s neon signs and ostentatious buildings recall more prosperous times. **Calle Bartolomé Masó** (also known as San Basilio), just behind Heredia and the cathedral, is a delightful street that leads down to the picturesque Tivolí district.

In Tivolí you'll find the famous **Padre Pico** steps, named for a Santiaguero priest who aided the city's poor. Castro once roared fire and brimstone down on the Batista government here, but today you'll find more pacific chess and domino players who have set up all-hours tables on the steps. Take the steps up to the **Museo de la Lucha Clandestina** (Museum of the Clandestine Struggle; charge; tel: 2262 4689). This excellent museum, in one of the city's finest colonial houses, focuses on the activities of the resistance movement under local martyr Frank País. Residents of Santiago were instrumental in supporting the Revolution, as were peasants in the Sierra Maestra. From the museum's balcony, there are tremendous views of Santiago and the bay (and, unfortunately, of plumes of pollution rising up from factories).

South of the museum is one of Santiago's best places to get sweaty in the evening. The **Casa de las Tradiciones**, a "cultural centre" in a large colonial mansion with a central courtyard (Calle Jesús Rabí), has live *trova* and dancing. Known locally as La Casona, it's great fun, and local people usually outnumber tourists.

AROUND SANTIAGO

A good place to get your bearings on the suburbs of the city is from the rooftop bar of the hotel Meliá Santiago, 3km (almost 2 miles) east of the city's centre.

Bacardí's bat

Bacardi moved its headquarters and production to Puerto Rico after the Revolution, and from there to Bermuda. But it was the fruit bats that nested in the rafters of the original rum factory in Santiago that gave Bacardi rum its world-famous bat logo.

Plaza de la Revolución

In the near distance you can make out the yellow **Moncada Barracks**, which Castro, along with around a hundred rebels attacked on July 26, 1953. The date is now a rallying cry and public holiday, and the barracks have been converted into a school and museum, known both as the **Antiguo Cuartel Moncada** and the **Museo Histórico 26 de Julio** (Avenida Moncada esq. Gen. Portuondo; charge; tel: 2266 1157).

The museum tells the story of the road to revolution using dozens of memorable photographs. Also on display are various bloodstained rebel uniforms, some of Fidel's personal effects from his time in the mountains and "26 Julio" armbands (sporting the name of the resistance movement that developed after the Moncada attack). The bullet holes over the entrance were "restored" from photos.

North of Moncada is the **Plaza de la Revolución**, an open square at the corner of Av. las Américas and Av. de los Libertadores. Massive machetes (used by *mambí* independence fighters) thrust towards the sky in this monument to Antonio Maceo, a hero of the war of independence, who is seen riding triumphantly.

Southwest, opposite the railway and bus station, is the **Museo del Ron** (charge; https://havana-club.com/en-gb/museum), a new small rum museum inside the old Bacardí rum factory. It contains a moderately interesting collection of antique machinery, displays, a chance to see the factory at work producing Ron Caney, and a rum tasting.

The fine **Cementerio Santa Ifigenia** (charge; tel: 2263 1626), just north of the harbour (Av. Crombet, Reparto Juan Gómez), is the resting place of many Cuban heroes. The tombs to receive the most visitors, though, are those of Fidel Castro (1926–2016), whose ashes are interred in a simple boulder with a plaque marked simply "Fidel", and of José Martí, whose vast octagonal mausoleum was designed so that the tomb catches the sun throughout the day. The two are close together and if visiting them it is worth waiting for the changing of the guard every half an hour, accompanied by martial music.

Seven kilometres (4 miles) from the city is the seventeenth-century **Castillo del Morro**, surveying the harbour mouth from a commanding clifftop position and now a UNESCO World Heritage

View from Castillo del Morro

Basílica del Cobre

Site housing exhibits on piracy (charge; tel: 2269 1569). Moated, thick-walled and full of cannons, drawbridges and passageways, it is in fine condition. A guide will point out a torture room with a trap door in the floor, through which uncooperative prisoners and slaves were reportedly dropped into the sea below. The easiest way to get to El Morro is to hire a taxi.

A place of great import (and considerable beauty) is the triple-domed **Basílica del Cobre** ㉙ named after the nearby copper mines that rise out of the forested foothills 18km (11 miles) west of Santiago. Cuban faithfuls make annual pilgrimages to the church to pay tribute to its statue of the Virgen de la Caridad (Virgin of Charity), Cuba's patron saint. According to legend, in 1606 three young fishermen struggling in their storm-tossed boat out in the bay were saved by the miraculous appearance of the Virgin, who was holding a mulatto baby Jesus in one hand and a cross in the other. Pilgrims, often making the last of the trek on their knees, pray to her image and place mementos and offerings of thanks for her miracles; among them are small boats and prayers for those who have tried to escape Cuba on rafts. Except during Mass, the Virgin is kept on the second floor, encased in glass and cloaked in a glittering gold robe.

Day trips are offered by tour operators in Santiago up into the Sierra Maestra. Some go to **El Saltón**, a picturesque waterfall in the grounds of a small hotel. Alternatively, you can hike up Pico

Turquino (1,974m/6,476ft), the highest mountain, or visit Fidel's rebel HQ, **La Comandancia de la Plata**, near Santo Domingo. West, along the coast, you can dive to see shipwrecks, the remains of ships from the 1898 Spanish-American war. Ask at tour operators in town.

East of Santiago the Sierra de La Gran Piedra rises majestically above the coast. A tortuous side road 12km (7 miles) east along the coast ascends the mountains to **La Gran Piedra ㉚** (Great Stone), where you can climb on foot for a bird's-eye view of eastern Cuba. About 2km (1 mile) beyond, a track leads to the **Cafetal-Museo La Isabelica**, a nineteenth-century coffee-plantation *finca* (country house). The museum is part of the UNESCO World Heritage Site that protects the architectural legacy of early nineteenth-century coffee farms.

GUANTÁNAMO PROVINCE

You can reach Cuba's remote, mountainous, far-eastern region from Santiago. The US military base of Guantánamo is synonymous with the "war against terror", and while there's no immediately obvious reason to visit Guantánamo itself, it is a pleasant, well-kept provincial

"GITMO"

Guantánamo, known to American military personnel as "Gitmo", is a curious anomaly in revolutionary Cuba. Where in the world is the US less likely to have a military base? Established in 1903 – making it the oldest overseas American naval base – the lease was effectively forced on the Cubans by an interventionist US administration. The US still sends its annual rent cheques (about US$4,000), which haven't been cashed since 1960. To do so would be to recognize the legitimacy of the American presence in Cuba.

town. The province has only one true tourist draw, but it's a super one: the magical little town of Baracoa.

BARACOA

The dry, cactus-strewn landscape of the south coast begins to change as you follow the winding, spectacular 30km (18-mile) road "La Farola" across the mountains to **Baracoa** ㉛ (150km/93 miles from Santiago), a small, picturesque city known for its local chocolate and coconut factories. The tropical seaside town is surrounded by green hillsides covered with cocoa and coconut groves, and all around are palm-backed beaches. Baracoa lies smack in the middle of the wettest region in Cuba, with almost thirty rivers, most of them ripe for whitewater rafting. In the mountains to the northwest is the Parque Nacional Alejandro de Humboldt, a biosphere reserve named after the great German naturalist and explorer.

Baracoa was the first settlement to be established by Diego Velázquez in 1511. Columbus came here first, though, after landing at Bariay Bay in today's Holguín province in October 1492, and planted the Cruz de la Parra (Cross of the Vine) in the soil on his arrival. What is claimed to be this cross is on display in **Nuestra Señora de la Asunción**, the church on Plaza Independencia.

The town has suffered major hurricane damage in recent years, particularly on the seafront Malecón, but always picks itself up.

A good place to get your bearings is the hilltop *Hotel El Castillo*, a former castle looking out over red-tiled roofs,

Festive day

Baracoa really shines the week of April 1, when heady street parties every night commemorate the date General Antonio Maceo disembarked at nearby Playa Duaba in 1895, marking the beginning of Cuba's War of Independence.

Baracoa: the first Spanish settlement on Cuba, famous for its food and adventures

the town's expansive, oyster-shaped bay and the landmark mountain called El Yunque (The Anvil), named for its singular shape.

In the main square is a bust of Hatuey, the brave Indigenous Taíno leader who resisted early *conquistadores* until he was caught by the Spanish and burned at the stake. There's also a very lively Casa de la Trova here. It is worth wandering along the Malecón, the seaside avenue, from the snug **Fuerte Matachín**, an early nineteenth-century fort that has a small but informative municipal museum inside (free; tel: 2164 2122) to the *Hotel La Rusa*, which is named after a legendary Russian émigré who over the years hosted celebrities such as Che Guevara and Errol Flynn.

In and around Baracoa are several dozen pre-Columbian archaeological sites related to the two major Indigenous groups that once inhabited the region. The **Museo Arqueológico** (charge) in **La Cueva del Paraíso** up the hill from the village, contains a copy of the Taíno tobacco idol found nearby in 1903 (the original is in Havana).

Local musicians in Havana

THINGS TO DO

ENTERTAINMENT

Although cultural activity has been under state control since the Revolution and Havana no longer sizzles with the sleazy Mafia-funded casinos and clubs of the 1950s, both high culture and down-to-earth nightlife thrive in Cuba. Outside the resorts, it can be hard to pin down what's going on where, but informal musical performances are ubiquitous, on most streets you're likely to see something. In the resorts, nightlife is focused around hotels, ranging from decent live bands, dance and fashion shows to Beatles sing-alongs.

LIVE MUSIC PERFORMANCES

Cubans crave live music, and – with the surge in international popularity of traditional Cuban music – so do most visitors to Cuba. You certainly won't have to go out of your way to hear music performances. Roving groups of musicians can be found playing everywhere from airports to restaurants. Merely wandering the streets of Havana, Santiago or Trinidad, you're likely to stumble across a live band, or even a back alley where some impromptu jamming is going on.

All the styles of Cuba's traditional music – *habaneras, son, boleros, guarachas, guajiras* and more – can be heard in every town's *casa de la trova*, usually a fine old building on or near the main square. Performances take place afternoons and evenings. Especially in the evenings and on weekends, the island's *casas de la trova* really swing. The most famous is in Santiago de Cuba, while those in towns like Trinidad, Baracoa, Camagüey and Holguín are great fun.

Getting the salsa rhythm

Aside from traditional acoustic music, Cuba revels in salsa. In Havana the salsa dance fan can choose from a number of venues pretty much every night. Venues feature top salsa groups, but the cover charges are still quite low. Music hotspots include:

Havana. *Casa de la Música* (all types of music and dance including salsa; Avenida 35 and Calle 20, Miramar; www.facebook.com/casadelamusica miramar), *Casa de la Música Habana* (lots of variety from rock to salsa, new bands and established big names; Calle Galiano 255, e/ Concordia y Neptuno, Centro; www.facebook.com/casa musicahabana), Teatro Nacional (5th floor, Paseo y Calle 39, Plaza de la Revolución) for *Café Cantante* (dancing to live bands or disco, often top bands in the basement; www.facebook.com/ CafeCantanteMiHabana), *La Fábrica de Arte Cubano* (Calle 26 esq. 11, el Vedado; www.fac.cu) and alfresco nights at *Club Jardines del 1830* (Malecón 1252 esq. 20).

Trinidad. *Casa de la Trova* (traditional Cuban music; Fernando Echerri 29, e/ Jesús Menéndez y Patricio Lumumba) and *Casa de la Música* (www.facebook.com/CasaMusicaTrinidad) on the Escalinata near the Plaza Mayor, *Rincón de la Salsa* (Calle Rosario) and *Palenque de los Congos Reales* (Afro-Cuban folkloric show during the day; Fernando Echerri half a block away towards the Plaza Mayor).

Santiago de Cuba. *Casa de la Trova* (*trova*, *son* and boleros, famous musicians play here; Calle Heredia), *Casa de las Tradiciones* (*trova*, *son* and boleros; Calle Rabí 154).

Baracoa. *Casa de la Trova* (Calle Felix Ruene) and *Casa de la Cultura* (Maceo, 124).

A MUSICAL MELTING POT

Salsa, rumba, mambo, *cha-cha-chá*, *son*, *danzón* – Cuba's rhythms are known the world over. Reflecting the mixed heritage of its people, Cuban music exploded towards the end of the 1800s through the nexus of African and European cultures – in particular what's been described as the love affair between the African drum and the Spanish guitar. In a typical Cuban band today you'll hear Latin stringed instruments in harmony with congas, *timbales* and African bongos (all drums), *claves* (wooden sticks) and instruments made from hollow gourds such as the maracas and the *güiro*. Cuban percussionists are among the finest in the world.

First came *son* (sound), a style that originated in el Oriente around the turn of the twentieth century. *Son* permeates all Cuban music and is the direct forebear of salsa; it has a percussive swing that is intrinsically Cuban. Mixed with jazz influences, it led to the brass-band salsa of famous groups such as Los Van Van, Isaac Delgado and Irakere. *Cha-cha-chá* arrived in the 1950s, having developed from mambo, itself a blend of jazz and the sedate, European *danzón* of the ballroom. The strongly Afro-Cuban rumba is typified by heavy drumming and more celebratory, erotic dancing. *Trovas* (ballads) were sung in colonial times by troubadors in *casas de la trova*. After the revolution the *trova* evolved into the *nueva trova*, often with overtly political lyrics, made popular by such artists as Silvio Rodríguez and Pablo Milanés.

CABARET

A legacy of the high-rolling casino days in Cuba, cabarets have been kept alive and well as a magnet for tourist spending.

While the best shows at the **Tropicana** clubs in both Havana and Santiago de Cuba (www.cabaret-tropicana.com) are rather expensive by Cuban standards, seeing at least one big song-and-dance production is de rigueur.

The **Tropicana in Havana** (Calle 72 e/ 45 y Línea de Ferrocarril, Marianao) founded in 1939, is indisputably the queen of cabarets. The likes of Nat King Cole performed here in pre-revolutionary times. With a 32-piece orchestra and a cast of over two hundred, in a dazzling open-air arena, the sheer scale of the spectacle will make your head spin. Tickets cost from US$75, including a quarter bottle of rum and a mixer. Book online or at your hotel reception. The show starts at 10pm and lasts 1 hour 45 minutes, after which you can head to the club. Havana's next-best cabaret show, smaller and half the price, is *Cabaret Parisien*, at the *Hotel Nacional* (Calles 21 and O, Vedado; https://hotelnacionaldecuba.com).

Cabaret Las Vegas (Calzada de la Infanta 104) is a gay club that hosts regular drag (*transformistas*) shows – Reinas de la Noche (tel: 7836 7939).

The **Tropicana in Santiago de Cuba** (Autopista Nacional Km 1.5) fills an enormous complex on the city's northern outskirts. It is no less impressive than Havana's but tickets are much less expensive.

DANCE

Afro-Cuban dance is often seen in resort hotels as part of the evening entertainment, but is best seen in theatres or live. Head to Callejón de Hamel (Centro Habana) on Sunday at noon for rumba and more. The Conjunto Folklórico Nacional de Cuba perform at UNEAC in el Vedado, Teatro América in Centro and more venues.

Tropicana Cabaret performer, Havana

Check their social media page for events (www.insta gram.com/conjuntofolk loriconacdecuba).

The Ballet Nacional de Cuba was created in 1961 and has been supported by the Revolution ever since. It is under the direction of Viengsay Valdés who took over the direction from the late prima ballerina Alicia Alonso (see page 37). World famous and often on tour, when in Cuba they perform at the Gran Teatro on the Parque Central, Havana or the Teatro Nacional, Plaza de la Revolución (www.balletcuba.cult.cu). The Ballet de Camagüey is another classical ballet company, sometimes considered to be more innovative. Also worth seeing is Danza Contemporánea de Cuba (www.instagram.com/danzacontemporaneadecuba), which is based at the Teatro Nacional but also performs at other venues in Havana and nationwide.

Visitors to Santiago de Cuba should try to see the very talented Ballet Folklórico Cutumba, a renowned troupe that delves into the world of Afro-Cuban spirituality and ritual. They perform at several theatres when in town and also offer dance classes. Visit Paradiso agency (Heredia 302 esq. Carnicería) to get the lowdown.

OTHER DANCE VENUES
Situated in an old peanut oil factory, trendy *Fabrica de Arte Cubano* (Calle 26 esq. 11, Vedado; www.instagram.com/fabrica

deartecubano) offers a unique blend of art, music, cinema, disco and dance – expect long queues. *La Gruta*, on Calle 23, is a long-standing salsa dancing option. *Club 500* (Calle 12 e/3ra y Calzada) hosts salsa and disco nights and big names take to the state at the *Salón Capri*, part of el Vedado's *Hotel Capri*. Newer venues include *Bar Salsa Habana* (Habana 416 e/ Obispo y Obrapía; www.facebook.com/barsalsahabana). Varadero has a popular *Casa de la Música* (www.facebook.com/CasaMusicaVaradero). In Trinidad, the *Discoteca Ayala Las Cuevas* really gets going at 1am, when the other music venues in town close. Salsa aficionados should visit Cuba for its annual Festival de la Salsa (www.facebook.com/FestivalDeLaSalsaEnCuba/#).

Finding out what's on for dance nights and live music nights isn't easy. The best option is to check out Havana Edge while you're on the road (www.facebook.com/HavanaEdge) – you'll find rock, salsa, DJs and reggaeton nights listed here.

BARS AND CAFÉS

Both bars and cafés are places to have a mojito, daiquiri or shot of *ron* (rum), smoke a Cohiba and – usually – hear some live Cuban rhythms. In Havana the classic bar not to miss is Hemingway's *El Floridita* (see page 37). Other places to tap into the zeitgeist are *Bar Yarini* in Old Havana with music nights, *El del Frente*'s rooftop bar, and the bar-cafés of Plaza Vieja. In Centro Havana, head to *La Guarida*'s rooftop bar for drinks and music, *Malecón 663* for musical acts all week, and *El Bleco* is for late nights with DJ sets. In el Vedado, look up *Hotel Claxon*'s musical roster – Las noches de Fangio. Its jazz nights are popular. *EFE Bar* is for DJS and late nights on Calle 23 (www.facebook.com/efebarcuba).

In Santa Clara you'll find *Club el Mejunje*, an LGBTQ+ champion and cultural venue with excellent live music and theatre, and *Café-Museo Revolucíon* which is stuffed with Che memorabilia.

Preparing mojitos in the bar of Hotel Nacional

In Camagüey, visit *Bar el Cambio* and you'll be served a stonking mojito.

In Santiago de Cuba, the terrace bar on the fifth floor of the *Hotel Casa Granda* has fine views and live music. At the corner of Calle Calvario is *Café Isabelica*, a venerable 24-hour bohemian haunt in a house three centuries old. The atmospheric rum bar next to the new Museo de Ron hosts live music.

CLASSICAL REPERTOIRE

The classical arts are greatly valued in Cuba, and drama, opera, classical music recitals and above all ballet can be enjoyed in theatres all around Cuba. Opulent, old-fashioned theatres such as those in Cienfuegos, Camagüey and Matanzas and Havana's magnificent Gran Teatro, are sights in their own right.

The Gran Teatro Alicia Alonso in Havana, at Prado y San José (www.facebook.com/www.granteatro.cu), has two main concert halls and puts on a wide repertoire of entertainment, from opera recitals to ballet. It is home to the internationally renowned Ballet Nacional de Cuba. Havana's International Ballet Festival is held every two years during the last week of October and first week of November.

Other theatres and concert halls include the small Sala de Conciertos space in the Cuban section of the Museo de Bellas Artes, Teatro Martí in Old Havana, and the San Francisco Convent. A comprehensive lowdown can be found here: http://habanacultural.ohc.cu/?page_id=22.

In el Vedado venues include the *Sala Hubert de Blanck*, for classical and contemporary music concerts as well as drama and dance; Teatro El Sótano, for contemporary drama, Teatro Ciervo Encantado for avant-garde works, Teatro Mella for modern dance and drama and Teatro Nacional de Cuba for concerts. Out in Miramar is the Teatro Karl Marx, used for grand occasions when large audiences can be accommodated. For events of all types and across all provinces consult http://lapapeleta.cu.

Export permits

If you purchase anything that can be described as art – even a cheap watercolour at a flea market – you'll need an official export permit to get it out of the country without hassle or fear of confiscation. Most galleries and outlets should be able to provide you with this – a purchase receipt will not usually be sufficient.

SHOPPING

Cuba has a reputation as a destination where there's little worth buying. You will see incredibly barren shops – window displays with bottles of cooking oil, shoe polish and a few plumbing parts, large state-run shops selling tinned foods and detergent where goods are bought via MLC (hard currency cards) or

foreign bank cards, and new privately run kiosks/stores selling food and drink following new laws introduced in 2021. There are plenty of souvenirs and crafts for visitors to buy, too. Top on most people's lists are cigars, rum and art. There is also an excellent selection of handicrafts, and tourist markets are now thriving in Cuba's major centres, even if much of what you'll find is related to Che Guevara – berets, T-shirts bearing his countenance and dolls, among many other "revolutionary" items. The last ten years have seen a surge in private spaces selling designer souvenirs, crafts and clothes.

For essentials, hotel stores and dollar shops (aka MLC stores) carry mineral water, soap, shampoo, toilet paper and toothpaste, and sometimes mosquito repellent and suncream. However, it's still best to bring all your medicinal or cosmetic staples from home; medicines are in short supply. It's also best to bring a water bottle with a filter.

SOUVENIRS TO BUY

Cigars and rum. The biggest bargain in Cuba is probably a coveted box of premium cigars, which at home might cost four times more. Cigar factories have affiliated shops selling all brands of cigars; the original Partagás factory in Havana has a particularly good shop, as does the specialist cigar hotel in Old Havana:

Cuba's fine cigars

Hostal Conde de Villanueva at Mercaderes 202. You can purchase cigars at any official Casa del Habano store, they are also at larger hotels and at airports around the country.

Bottles of Cuban **rum** also offer big savings. All tourist shops sell rum, whether aged from three to seven years *(añejo)* or low-grade *aguardiente* (from sugar-cane alcohol) with humorous labels. Havana Club is the brand of choice and aficionados should visit the distillery's Museo del Ron (charge; https://havana-club.com/en-gb/museum) for a tour and rum tasting, as well as the shop attached. Above *El Floridita*, Havana's *Casa del Ron* has the most impressive selection of rums, including hundred-dollar vintages.

Handicrafts. Local arts and crafts vary from tacky figurines to drawings of street scenes. You'll also find evocative posters and black-and-white photos of Fidel, Che and company. Fine handmade lace and crochet are available, principally in Trinidad. You might want to pick up a *guayabera*, the classic Cuban pleated, four-pocketed man's shirt, worn untucked. Quitrín (Obispo esq. San Ignacio in Old Havana) has the nicest cotton versions of the original white *guayabera*. Much of the silver-plated jewellery is also a good buy, but you should not purchase anything with black coral – it's endangered and illegal to import in many countries.

EL PURO: THE CUBAN CIGAR

Before launching the US trade embargo against Cuba, President Kennedy reportedly had an aide round up a supply of his favourite Cuban cigars. Now that cigars have again become chic, almost everyone knows that Cuban *puros* are reputed to be the world's finest. Factories produce more than 350 million cigars a year, with 100 million for export. Before the Revolution there were more than a thousand Cuban brands of cigars; today there are only about three dozen.

You can visit a number of cigar factories, where the rich aroma is overwhelming. *Torcedores* wrap the different types of leaves (some for taste, burn, etc) inside the wrapper leaves with dexterous ease. Sacks of tobacco leaves are sorted into bundles, cigars undergo quality control tests, and prestigious labels are applied. Handmade cigars vary in length from the 4.5-inch Demi Tasse to the 9.25-inch Gran Corona. As a rule, bigger cigars are of better quality and darker-coloured cigars taste sweeter. Back home, keep your cigars moist: place them in a humidor or put the box in a plastic bag with a damp sponge.

Buying a box of cigars can be daunting. People on the street will whisper "You want cigar, my friend?" – they may be hot, but they may also be inferior-quality fakes. Don't buy unless you know what you're doing.

Fakes are liable to confiscation by customs. In official shops, make sure you keep the two copies of the official receipt – one of these is for you and one is to be given to customs when leaving the country. Keep cigars in your hand luggage for inspection. You are allowed to take up to twenty loose cigars and up to fifty in their original sealed packaging, with the official hologram, out of the country without a receipt.

In Havana, find the lively craft market Almacenes San José (closed Mon) on the port road. For designer souvenirs, head to women-run Clandestina (https://clandestina.co), Dador for fashion (www.dadorhavana.com), Beyond Roots championing Black culture for souvenirs (https://beyondroots.net), Alma for beautiful handcrafts sourced from around the country (www.almacubashop.com), Piscolabis for many wonderful crafts and a few higher end pieces (www.facebook.com/PiscolabisLaHabana), Memorias for antique and historical pieces, old posters, postcards, books and coins (http://tiendamemorias.com/en) in addition to the second-hand book and curios market (see page 31), tattoo studio La Marca for art, clothes and graphics (www.instagram.com/lamarcabodyarthavana), Cicloecopapel (https://cicloecopapel.ola.click) for recycled paper craft and cards, and to Casa y Limón (www.instagram.com/casaylimon) for homewares.

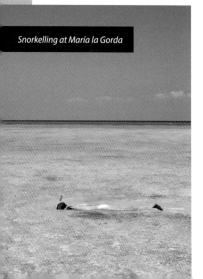

Snorkelling at María la Gorda

For serious art, check out the studios of Cuban artists as well as official galleries. The best aid for this is to buy the book *Cutting Edge Art in Havana: 100 Cuban Artists.*

In Santiago, the Galería René Valdés houses a collection of arts and crafts (www.facebook.com/galeria renevaldes) and along Calle Heredia you'll find a wonderful memorabilia store and artists selling art and crafts. In Camagüey, seek out the artists' studios in the city (see page 71) and in Trinidad, there are dozens of arts and craft shops and stalls with ceramics, woodwork and lacework being prized items.

Music You can still find music sold in official stores on the island, and local musicians sell their own CDs at bars and cafés. Most artists have gone digital, now.

SPORTS

WATERSPORTS

Watersports enthusiasts are in luck in Cuba. Virtually every resort offers windsurfing, sailing, scuba diving and snorkelling. Watersports centres are almost always affiliated with a particular hotel, but anyone may rent the equipment.

Diving and **snorkelling** are of great interest. Cuba claims to be surrounded by one of the world's largest coral reefs, and over a thousand sunken wrecks. Facilities are generally ok but not superb. Nearly every resort has at least one professional diving centre equipped with all the requisite equipment. Most centres offer week-long diving courses for an internationally recognized qualification, as well as introductory courses. Serious divers should bring as much of their own equipment as possible. All travellers should bring their own mask and snorkel.

Dozens of dive sites can be reached from resorts, typically a half-hour boat journey away. Resorts catering to all levels of ability include Playa Santa Lucía, María la Gorda, Cayo Levisa, Cayo Largo, Varadero, Playa Girón, Playa Ancón, Gardens of the King and Guardalavaca. The outstanding Gardens of the Queen is a three-hour boat ride from the south coast with one-week liveaboard options or a floating hotel only (https://cubandiving centers.com).

Deep-sea fishing is one of Cuba's great attractions, yet not well-known (or over-fished). Trips in search of marlin, wahoo, swordfish and tarpon or smaller fry can be arranged through **Marlin Naútica y Marinas** around the island at the Marina Hemingway, Marina Tarará, Varadero, Cayo Guillermo, Cayo Coco, Santa Lucía, Guardalavaca, Marina Santiago de Cuba, Marina Trinidad, Marina Cienfuegos, Jardines de la Reina, Isla de la Juventud and Cayo Largo del Sur. There is fly fishing in the Jardines de la Reina off the south coast, off Cayo Largo del Sur and in the salt flats of the Zapata Peninsula (https://cubanfishingcenters.com/jardines-de-la-reina.php). For **freshwater fishing**, Hanabanilla and Zaza (near Sancti Spíritus) lakes both hold impressively big, copious large-mouth bass, as do Maspotón in Pinar del Río, Laguna del Tesoro in the Zapata Peninsula.

SPECTATOR SPORTS

The national sport is **baseball** (béisbol). Cuban teams are among the best in the world (several stars have defected to the US major leagues). While children improvise with a stick and a makeshift ball in every town's open spaces, the main cities have vast stadiums.

CUBA FOR CHILDREN

At resorts, water-loving babies will be happy; those aged 10 and up will be able to join in many of the activities. A growing number of resort hotels have children's clubs, and top hotels can arrange babysitting. Outside the resorts facilities are limited and transport can be problematic. Cubans adore children and will certainly make a fuss over yours. Travelling with young families in Cuba can be a remarkable – and eye-opening – experience. If you travel with very young children, be sure to take all the nappies and baby food you require, as these items are hard to find in Cuba. If travelling by hire car, you should supply your own car seat.

WHAT'S ON

The website www.cuba.travel/Eventos has information and contact details for all of the festivals and events held throughout the year all over the country. The Paradiso cultural agency (www.facebook.com/paradiso.cuba) is often the gateway for ticketed events for foreigners.

January New Year (January 1, public holiday): marked throughout the country and taking in Liberation Day, marking the end of the Batista dictatorship. International Jazz Plaza Festival: a week-long festival, which attracts top jazz artists from Cuba and around the world: performances, workshops, lectures and open rehearsals in Havana, Santiago and other cities (www.facebook.com/festivaljazzplazacuba).

February Annual cigar festival held in Havana (www.habanos.com/en).

May May Day (May 1, public holiday): a big event with parades and speeches in Havana's Plaza de la Revolución.

May or June Hemingway Marlin Fishing Tournament (Hemingway Marina, Havana).

July (first week): Caribe Festival (Santiago de Cuba): street parades, concerts, lectures and fairs celebrating Afro-Caribbean culture (www.festivaldelcaribe.net).

July *Carnaval* (Santiago de Cuba) in late July: Cuba's most famous celebration, featuring *comparsas* (street dances); takes in Santiago's patron saint's day on the 25th, but stops temporarily on the 26th in memory of the attack on the Moncada barracks in 1953.

August *Carnaval* (Havana): parades, open-air concerts and street parties.

September Fiesta de la Virgen del Cobre on September 8: pilgrimage to the altar of Cuba's saint in El Cobre near Santiago de Cuba.

October–November Havana International Ballet Festival: top ballet companies gather from around the world, every two years since 1960.

November–February The Havana art fair: held irregularly but it is an important event in the cultural calendar (www.wlam.cult.cu/bienal_de_la_habana.html#header3-aa).

December New Latin American Film Festival (Havana): the most important film festival in Latin America, held during the first two weeks of the month.

FOOD AND DRINK

It is a sad paradox that a land as fertile as Cuba should have such problems feeding its people. During the so-called Special Period of the early 1990s and since Covid-19, food shortages have become serious. Ration books no longer provide enough to live on leaving poor Cubans with uncertainty. However, those with plenty of money (tourists and a number of Cubans) are immune from hardships and get the most and best of what is available (Cuba imports 80 percent of its food). Cuba once had a respectable *criollo* (Creole) cuisine, a fusion of Spanish and African culinary traditions, but many state restaurants have no choice but to offer standard "chicken or pork" main courses, along with rice and beans. *Paladares* (private restaurants) offer a whole variety of Cuban cuisine, Cuban cuisine with a twist, and international fare. It's here you'll find the best food. Most of the excellent *paladares* are found in Havana, with a scattering of highlights found around the island.

WHERE TO EAT

If you're based in a resort, you might face the potentially monotonous reality of eating almost all your meals at the hotel. Large hotels often have not only a main buffet restaurant but also an a la carte restaurant, a poolside *parrillada* (grill) and a beachside café.

State-run restaurants are of two types. There are cafeteria style restaurants with extremely limited menus that are, generally, of poor quality. And there are state-run restaurants you'll find in hotels and in big cities that vary from the desultory to fairly good.

Since the government allowed non-agricultural co-operatives, a number of restaurants are run by these new cooperatives.

A fourth category is the *paladar*, a privately operated restaurant or café in a private home or other venue. In 1995 the government legalized *paladares*, only to subsequently tax or fine many of them almost out of existence. In late 2010 restrictions were relaxed in order to create jobs, allowing more to open and employ staff, and increasing the maximum legal number of place settings from twelve to fifty. This move created thousands of new places to eat across the country and this is where you will find the most delicious food in Cuba. *Paladares* can still be mom-and-pop restaurants in someone's home but many are now found in converted buildings. Prices and standards vary enormously. The greatest variety is found in Havana – restaurants, cafés, burger kiosks and ice cream parlours. New private bars also sell food ranging from pizzas and snacks to full menus.

Cuban food at a restaurant in Viñales

Rice, beans and fried plantains

New laws introduced in 2021 permitted small and medium-sized enterprises (mipymes) allowing private restaurants to import. Private small grocery stores also emerged selling high-end deli items and covetable edibles.

If you are staying at a *casa particular* (see page 112), take advantage of the freshest and best *criollo* food if you're offered it. Usually, you'll need to decide in the morning whether you want to eat in, and they will shop and cook it for your evening meal. Fortified by a hearty breakfast of fresh fruit, eggs, coffee, juice and bread, these two meals will probably be enough for the day, with just a snack at midday. *Casas particulares* that offer breakfast now charge extra.

In all resort hotels and around Havana, state cafés serve sandwiches (almost always ham and/or cheese) and coffee, but otherwise snacks in Cuba are generally street pizza, sandwiches, pastries, sweets and churros. At private farmers' markets (*agromercados*) you will find fruit and veg.

WHAT TO EAT

At hotels and in the resorts, breakfast is often a buffet of fresh fruit, fruit juices, cheeses, meats, yoghurts, pancakes and egg dishes made to order. In more modest hotels, sandwiches and omelettes are generally the staple fare.

Hotel buffets are also offered at lunch and dinner, and guests with large appetites will find these very good value. The food is "international" rather than typically Cuban. The surfeit of choices (several salads, piles of bananas, chunks of watermelon, cakes galore, a choice of fish, meat and pasta) might make some travellers uncomfortable, given the limited supplies most Cubans put up with.

Most restaurants serve a Creole Cuban cuisine. Its main staple is rice and beans; you'll find either rice with kidney beans (*moros y cristianos*; "Moors and Christians") or rice with black beans (*congrí*), the latter typically served in the east of Cuba. Meat is often *pollo asado* (roast chicken) or *cerdo asado* (roast pork). White fish is commonly presented under the generic label *pescado* and is typically fresh and simply grilled; many restaurants also serve lobster at a hefty price. Popular side dishes include root vegetables such as *malanga* and *yuca* (cassava) in addition to *maduros* or *tostones* (fried plantains). Common desserts are *pasta de guayaba con queso* (cheese with guava paste), flan and ice cream. International fare is most commonly found in Havana. Regional cuisine is found predominantly in Baracoa.

WHAT TO DRINK

The national drink is *ron* (rum), produced from cane juice and molasses, the

Farmers market in Havana

Thirst-quencher: the mojito

by-products of sugar manufacture. Un-aged rum, called *aguardiente* ("firewater"), has a very high alcoholic content. Five- or seven-year-old rum, darkened and flavoured in oak barrels, is drunk straight or on the rocks.

Cuban cocktails make use of one- or three-year-old white rum. A number have achieved folkloric status: Hemingway drank his mojitos (sugar, lime juice, ice, fresh mint, rum and soda water) in *La Bodeguita del Medio* and his daiquiris (grapefruit juice, maraschino, lime juice and rum blended into crushed ice) in *El Floridita* (see page 37). Less exotic is the *Cuba libre*: simply rum and coke, served with a slice of lime. Craft cocktails are on the rise and you'll find them in the top, favourite bars of Havana, especially.

National brands of beer include Bucanero, Cristal, Mayabe and Tínima, all very drinkable.

For soft drinks, try the wonderfully sweet *guarapo* (pure sugar cane juice) or *granizado* (a flavoured water-ice in a paper cone from ubiquitous streetside carts).

Coffee is one of Cuba's main exports, but you don't always get export-quality coffee. In times of hardship it is mixed with chicory, a flavour many Cubans have got used to and now prefer. A *café* is served espresso style and traditionally drunk with unimaginable quantities of sugar; *café americano* is weaker and served in a large cup. *Café con leche* is half espresso/half milk.

TO HELP YOU ORDER...

Do you have a table? **¿Tiene una mesa?**
May I see the menu, please? **¿Puedo ver la carta, por favor?**
What do you recommend? **¿Qué me aconseja?**
I'd like … **Quisiera …**
I'm a vegetarian **Soy vegetariano.**

beer **la cerveza**
bread **el pan**
butter **la mantequilla**
cocktail **el cóctel**
coffee **el café**
dessert **el postre**
fish **el pescado**
fruit **fruta**
ice **el hielo**
ice cream **el helado**

meat **la carne**
salad **la ensalada**
sandwich **el bocadito**
shellfish **los mariscos**
soft drink **el refresco**
tea **el té**
vegetable **los vegetales/legumbres**
water **el agua mineral**
wine **el vino**

...AND READ THE MENU

arroz blanco white rice
asado roast/grilled
bistec steak
camarones shrimps/prawns
cerdo/puerco pork
congrí rice and beans
frijoles beans
frito fried
huevos eggs
jamón ham
jugo de fruta fruit juice

langosta lobster
naranja orange
pan tostado toast
papas potatoes
papas fritas chips (fries)
picadillo minced meat
platáno plantain
pollo chicken
queso cheese
tortilla/revoltillo omelette

WHERE TO EAT

We have used the following symbols to give an idea of the price for a three-course meal for one, excluding drinks, tips and shellfish (the latter is always the costliest on the menu).

$$$ over US$30
$$ US$15–30
$ under US$15

OLD HAVANA

Antojos $-$$ *Peña Pobre e/ Compostela y Habana, tel: 5282 4907.* This spot with great décor and atmosphere is deservedly popular for its delicious, beautifully presented Cuban cuisine dishes. Its *ropa vieja* is recommended. The cocktails are fantastic, too.

El Antonia $-$$ *Compostela 116 e/ Tejadillo y Empedrado, tel: 7860 3938.* A great place for light bites – wholesome cream of pumpkin soup boosted with ginger, tapas, pizzas and deeply delicious malanga fritters and croquetas. An electric roster of musicians – all known to the well-connected owner – keeps the place busy on nights of live music.

El Café $-$$ *Amargura 358 e/ Villegas y Aguacate, tel: 7861 3817.* This private café draws dozens of visitors for its breakfasts, delicious sourdough sandwiches, fruit shakes, pancakes, spot-on coffee and nice relaxed vibe.

El del Frente $-$$ *303 O'Reilly, Altos e/ Habana y Aguiar, tel: 5237 7533.* Salads, tacos, seafood and more at one of Havana's coolest spots. The alfresco roof terrace is for some serious drinking where double measures are applied. Great views in a busy area.

Ivan Chefs Justo $$$ *Aguacate 9, e/ Chacón y Tejadillo, tel: 7863 9697.* An upmarket *paladar* in a handsome eighteenth-century building is known for its meat and shellfish dishes. The memorable succulent roast suckling pig is the standout dish.

Jama $-$$ *Aguiar 261B e/ O'Reilly y Empedrado, tel: 5297 0745*. This wonderful spot serves up delicious sushi and a standout tuna tataki, with excellent cocktail options. Blending Cuban and Asian cuisine, there are tacos and more available at this downtown eatery.

Jíbaro $-$$ *Merced 69 e/ San Ignacio y Cuba, tel: 5284 9545*. This tiny restaurant and cocktail bar has all the vibes and great food – platters with a twist on Cuban cuisine. The owners help run a regular craft cocktail competition and run a fantastic street food tour.

Oasis Nelva $-$$ *Habana esq. Muralla, tel: 5638 2926*. A plant nursery and café serving up crepes, cassava tacos, organic vegetables, juices, locally made soft drinks, ice creams and great craft cocktails. An ideal spot for vegetarians.

Paco's Mar $$ *San Isidro esq. Cuba, tel: 5916 3131*. A great little find down in deepest Old Havana, this lovely diner is a winner on all fronts – pepped up Cuban food, drinks and service. Their tacos – beautifully presented – are legendary. Good seafood, too.

CENTRO

La Guarida $$$ *Calle Concordia, 418, e/ Gervasio y Escobar, tel: 5414 7852*. The most famous *paladar* in Havana, situated in the crumbling building where much of the Cuban film *Fresa y Chocolate* (1993) was filmed. The food is creative and wonderfully prepared, and there is occasionally live music at the rooftop bar.

Marechiaro $$ *Malecón 217 e/ Blanco y Aguila, tel: 5322 7006*. Italian-run restaurant with with gorgeous sea and sunset views. *Marechiaro* serves top-notch pizza, flavourful arancini, excellent raviolis and pizzas. Great coffee, too.

Tonyzzz $-$$ *Consulado esq. San Miguel, tel: 5442 7248*. Tony is from Sri Lanka. His melt-in-the-mouth chicken curry is rightly renowned at this low-key diner with a bar. It is a cosy venue and also serves some great vegetarian options.

EL VEDADO AND MIRAMAR

Camino al Sol $ *Calle 3 363 e/ Paseo y 2, tel: 7832 1861*. This small café is a vegetarian haven serving up fresh ravioli, pastas, tacos, salads and fruit shakes. It really is a treasure. There is food available to take away from the deli counter, too.

Grados $$$ *E 562 e/ 23 y 25, tel: 7833 7882*. Chef Raulito Bazuk's creative kitchen is always worth visiting. This fine diner (closed Mon and Tues) with lashings of magic delivers seriously tasty Cuban food. Be sure to try Bazuk's homemade cocktails, too!

Otramanera $$$ *1810 Avenida 35, tel: 7203 8315*. A superb fine diner in a modernist home serving up Havana's finest food, although closed Sun and Mon. Think Mediterranean food with a Cuban twist.

WESTERN CUBA

El Cajuaní $$–$$$ *Carretera El Moncada Km 2.2, Viñales, tel: 5882 8925*. Chef José serves up the freshest farm-to-table food at this cute clapboard home that sits prettily in front of a mogote.

El Galeon $$ *Calle 24 e/ 47 y 45 4510, Nueva Gerona, Isla de la Juventud, tel: 5350 9128*. There are very few places to eat on the Isle of Youth. This is the most popular restaurant in Nueva Gerona and it is always buzzing. You can expect solid *comida criolla*. The bar/café in the patio downstairs also serves pizza.

El Olivo $$ *Salvador Cisneros 89, Viñales, tel: 4869 6654*. This Mediterranean *paladar* is a welcome change from rice and beans. Good fish, pasta, paella and absolutely tons of wonderful goats' cheese from its own farm. The service is slow but the food is tasty.

El Romero $-$$ *Las Terrazas, tel: 4857 8700*. Established by Cuba's pioneering vegetarian chef, this lovely low-food-miles restaurant, with a balcony overlooking the community lake, serves up vegetarian food and juices. Nice view and a tranquil atmosphere.

VARADERO

Mansión Xanadú $$$ *Av. Las Américas, Km 8.5, tel: 4566 8482*. Grand seaside mansion serving international dishes with variable success. Lunchtime snacks available on the terrace. On the third floor the *Casa Blanca Panoramic Bar* has cocktails and live music.

Salsa Suarez $$–$$$ *Calle 31, tel: 5328 7678*. This smart restaurant is the best in Varadero with consistently excellent food and service. Come for the seafood and the desserts.

BAY OF PIGS

Chuchi El Pescador $-$$ *Caletón, Playa Larga, tel: 4598 7336*. A well-established *paladar* with a huge offering of seafood and comida criolla. It's right on the edge of the village of Caletón.

CIENFUEGOS

Villa Lagarto $$$ *Calle 35, Punta Gorda e/ 0 y Litoral, tel: 43 51 9966*. This long-standing *paladar* faces the water and serves up tasty *comida criolla* cuisine.

SANTA CLARA

El Alba $$ *Buen Viaje 26 e/ Maceo y Parque Vidal, tel: 4220 3935*. Grilled meats are the speciality at this Santa Clara *paladar*. There's plenty of seafood, too.

TRINIDAD

Muñoz Tapas $–$$ *Maceo 476A e/ Desengaño y Rosario*. A restaurant with a rooftop bar serving up everything from breakfasts to fruit juices to chicken and pork tacos, pizza and hamburgers as well as a full range of *comida criolla*.

San José $$$ *Maceo No. 382 entre Colon y Smith, tel: 5308 1733*. A top *paladar* in the city offering a large range of soups and snacks (the fried taro root with honey is delicious). It offers a huge menu of meats, fish and shellfish.

Taberna La Botija $$ *Calle Amargura esq. Boca, tel: 5522 2464*. The extensive taco menu here is a huge draw as is the *ropa vieja* made with shredded lamb. The tavern honours slave history with artefacts on the walls.

CAMAGÜEY

Hostal San Rafael $ *Plaza San Juan de Dios, tel: 3228 5541*. Delicious breakfasts, coffees, lunches and more at this small boutique hotel with an interior patio.

Méson del Príncipe $-$$ *Astilleros 18 e/ San Ramón y Lugareno; tel: 3227 4210*. A solid *paladar* offering up reasonably priced *comida criolla*. The grilled fish is great value.

SANTIAGO DE CUBA

El Madrileño $$ *Calle 8 105 e/ 3ra y 5ta, Vista Alegre, tel: 2264 4138*. A classic *paladar* in the patio of a Vista Alegre home serving up the highlights of *comida criolla* including chicken, pork and lamb dishes as well as a full scope of seafood. Great service.

El Palenquito $$-$$$ *Av del Río no. 28 between 6 and Carretera del Caney, Reparto Pastorita, tel: 2264 5220*. This garden ranch restaurant is on the edge of town but the trip is worth it for the best BBQ food in the city.

St Pauli $$ *Enramadas 605, close to Plaza Marte, tel: 5896 6055*. A longstanding *paladar* that always delivers. Although not the speediest service, *St Pauli* offers excellent *comida criolla* and always has a good range of seafood dishes.

BARACOA

Baracoando $ *Flor Crombet y Castillo Duany, La Punta, tel: 5258 9319*. Chef Aristides Smith's vegan restaurant is one of the best places to eat in all of Cuba. Fresh, organic platters incorporating regional cuisine traditions are served up in his hurricane-battered home.

TRAVEL ESSENTIALS

PRACTICAL INFORMATION

A

ACCOMMODATION

Standards and facilities have improved dramatically over the past few years. Cuba's new or restored hotels in beach resorts and in Havana typically have pools, restaurants, buffets, stores, air conditioning and satellite TV. Top resort hotels offer round-the-clock entertainment, while simpler resort hotels offer some in-house entertainment and invariably have a pool. Elsewhere, there are large, Soviet-style concrete eyesores located on the outskirts of towns, but there are now a number of small, attractive boutique hotels in town centres in renovated old hotels with plenty of character.

Casas particulares – private accommodation in Cuban homes – are inexpensive alternatives that can be the most rewarding way of experiencing Cuba. Not only do you get to know the owners, but there is usually a better standard of service, cleanliness and comfort than in the equivalent or higher value hotel room. *Casas particulares* must be registered with the authorities and should display a blue, anchor-shaped sign on or above the front door.

Outside such high periods as Christmas, New Year and Easter, you don't always need advance reservations, but it helps. For reservations from abroad it is worth checking www.airbnb.co.uk/cuba/stays.

I'd like a room with twin beds/double bed **Quisiera una habitación con dos camas/cama matrimonial**
What's the price? **¿Cuál es el precio?**
Is breakfast included? **¿El desayuno está incluído?**
Is there a private homestay near here? **¿Conoce una casa particular por aquí?**

AIRPORTS (see Getting there)

Cuba's main airport is Havana's José Martí International Airport, located 20km

(12 miles) south of downtown Havana. Varadero's Juan Gualberto Gómez Airport is 22km (14 miles) west of Varadero. Santiago de Cuba's Antonio Maceo Airport is located 6km (4 miles) south of that city. There are also international airports in Camagüey, Cayo Coco, Cayo Largo, Holguín, Santa Clara, Varadero, Cienfuegos, Santiago de Cuba and Manzanillo.

On arrival, if you're on a package holiday a **bus** will transfer you to your hotel. Independent travellers can book bus services through Víazul (https://viazul.wetransp.com) to the city bus terminal, or a Transtur Shuttle (www.rentcarcuba.com/en/pages/ver/shutle), US$5 to three Havana hotel zones, otherwise take a **taxi** to downtown Havana for US$25. It's a 40-minute trip from José Martí airport to central Havana. From Varadero airport to the beach hotels, take a taxi or Víazul.

B

BICYCLE HIRE

With the scarcity of public transport, many Cubans ride bikes. Most resorts have bikes and mopeds to hire. Many rental bikes are old and have few gears, and serious cyclists intending to tour the country should bring their bikes, as well as plenty of parts and spare tubes. New bike hire services with quality bikes in Havana include Ruta Bikes (www.rutabikes.com), women-led Velo Cuba (www.facebook.com/veloencuba) and e-bikes with Cubyke (cubyke.com). Alternatively, you could try a bike tour with a Canadian-based company WoWCuba (www.wowcuba.com), or UK company Cubanía (https://cubaniatravel.com).

BUDGETING FOR YOUR TRIP

Compared with the rest of Latin America, Cuba can be surprisingly expensive, but it compares well with the rest of the Caribbean.

Transport to Cuba. The airfare is likely to be your greatest expenditure, especially if coming from Europe or Asia. It's cheapest to travel outside of high season (Nov to April) or on a package tour.

Accommodation. Top hotels in Havana and major resorts are comparable to North America and Europe. In resorts, all-inclusive deals (meals, drinks and entertainment) can be a good option. Private houses *(casas particulares)* are generally inexpensive.

Meals and drinks. Eating out is rarely very expensive, about US$25–30 per person in a smartish restaurant, but there are many restaurants and *paladares* where you can eat well for around US$15. If you are going to drink wine, this puts the price up quite a lot. In a bar, beer costs around US$2–3, mojitos US$1–4, depending on location. Street snacks are very inexpensive.

Local transport. Urban public transport is cheap and improving but still crowded and inefficient. Taxis and *bicitaxis* are the best way to get about within cities and resorts; they are inexpensive.

Incidentals. Gifts like prestigious hand-rolled cigars are expensive, even if much cheaper than they are abroad.

C

CAMPING

There are official campsites in isolated locations all over the island, but they offer basic concrete huts rather than tents. In each major town ask for the Campismo office (www.campismopopular.cu) for local campsites, most of which are used by Cubans on holiday. There are also campsites, hotels or parking sites for tourists using camper vans, with water, power and waste disposal, dotted around the island. Book through Daiquiri Tours (www.daiquiritravel.com/home). Wild camping is now permitted in Cuba.

CAR HIRE

Hiring a car in Cuba can be expensive and buying petrol (gasoline) is a bit problematic as only certain service stations will fill T-plates (tourist cars). Petrol for tourist cars – *especial* – can only be bought with bank cards (not connected to the US) or with a pre-paid USD Clásica Card bought from an exchange bureau, CADECA (www.cadeca.cu/es/content/venta-de-tarjetas-prepago-en-moneda-libremente-convertible). Petrol *especial* is now US$1.30/litre. State-run rental firms are often inefficient and difficult to deal with in the event of car damage or other problems. If you wish to hire a car in one place and return it in another, you pay an additional premium. To hire a car, you must be at least 21 and have had two years' driving experience, and you will need a national or international licence. You will need to bring car seats for young children. An additional driver is a few extra dollars a day. That additional driver can be a Cuban.

Cuba has none of the major international rental agencies. All car hire is done through state-run agencies such as Cubacar, REX and Havanautos. However, the easiest and most reliable third-party agency is Novela Cuba (https://novelacuba.com/en/car-rentals) with an office in Cuba and 24/7 customer service. A car with a driver can also be arranged. A car is rented with a full tank of petrol and there is no need to return it full. Rates begin at around US$90 per day for unlimited mileage and insurance included. Inspect the car before you set off to identify existing dents and scratches, and read the FAQs carefully.

I'd like to rent a car for a day/a week **Quisiera alquilar un auto/ carro por un día/una semana**
Fill it up. **Llénelo, por favor.**

CLIMATE

Cuba has a subtropical climate: hot and humid. The chart below shows the average daily temperature in Havana. For beach lovers and sightseers, November to May is the ideal time to visit, though there is plenty of sunshine year-round. Hurricane season lasts from June until the end of November. The more active should avoid the height of summer, when it's debilitatingly hot and wet. The mountains are cooler and the south and east drier and warmer. El Oriente can be wickedly hot – much hotter than the western region.

	J	F	M	A	M	J	J	A	S	O	N	D
°C	22	22	23	25	26	27	28	28	27	26	24	22
°F	72	72	73	77	79	81	82	82	81	79	75	72

CLOTHING

During the day you'll rarely need more than shorts or a skirt and a T-shirt (and swimsuit). At night in winter, a light sweater or jacket may be needed. In upmarket hotels, restaurants and nightclubs you are required to dress smart casual.

CRIME AND SAFETY (see also Emergencies and Police)

Cuba is a remarkably safe place in which to travel – one of the safest anywhere. The crime that does exist is generally directed at possessions rather than people, so place temptation out of sight. Most top hotels and many *casas particulares* provide safes.

In Havana, be sensible and take the same precautions you would in any unfamiliar city. At night keep to busy and well-lit streets (or walk in the middle of the road if there is no street lighting). There is much less crime outside the capital, but in Santiago you must take the same precautions as you would in Havana.

> I want to report a theft. **Quiero denunciar un robo.**
> my wallet/handbag/passport **mi cartera/bolso/pasaporte**
> safe (deposit box) **la caja fuerte**

D

DRIVING

Road conditions. There is little traffic outside of town centres. Most main roads are paved and in fairly good condition, although they are not well signposted. The Autopista Nacional (motorway) runs from Havana west to Pinar del Río and east to Jatibonico, just before Ciego de Avila. From there a good road heads east to Santiago de Cuba. A number of rural roads are not paved. Beware of potholes: some are big enough to cause real damage. Other hazards are cyclists, hidden railway crossings (where you must halt even if it looks unused) and wandering livestock. Driving at night is not advisable; Cubans often drive with headlights on full beam and animals may wander onto the road.

Rules and regulations. To drive, you must be 21 and have a valid driver's licence. Drive on the right. Speed limits, strictly enforced, are 100km/h (62mph) on the highway (motorway), 90km/h (56mph) on other open roads, 60km/h (37mph) on smaller rural roads and 40km/h (25mph) in urban areas. You are likely to get an on-the-spot fine if caught breaking the speed limit. Insurance is mandatory, as is wearing seatbelts. It's common practice to sound your horn when passing to let vehicles without rearview mirrors know what's happening.

Fuel (*gasolina*). Servi-Cupet stations are spread throughout the country and are open 24-hours. They are not self-service. Petrol or diesel must be paid for via bank card or Tarjeta Clásica, see page 114. The quality of regular petrol is poor, and rental companies insist you purchase expensive '*especial*' fuel. Make sure you have a list of stations that will service T-plate cars (tourist cars).

stop **pare**
caution **cuidado**
no parking **no parqueo**
give way (yield) **ceda el paso**
one-way **dirección única**
danger **peligro**
car registration papers **permiso de circulación**
driver's licence **licencia de manejar**
How do I get to … ? **¿Cómo se puede ir a … ?**
Is this the right street for … ? **¿Es ésta la calle que va a … ?**
Full tank, please. **Llénelo, por favor.**
My car has broken down. **Mi carro tiene problemas mecánicos.**
I have a flat tire. **Tengo la goma ponchada.**
May I park here? **¿Se puede aparcar acá?**
Is this the highway (road) to … ? **¿Es ésta la carretera hacia … ?**

E

ELECTRICITY

Electrical appliances in hotels and *casas particulares* operate on either 110 volts or 220 volts. Most outlets accept flat-pin plugs, some round-pin plugs. Take an adapter. Blackouts are common in Cuba. Bring a portable battery back-up and torch.

What's the voltage? **¿Cuál es el voltaje?**
adaptor/a battery **un adaptador/una pila**

EMBASSIES

Canada: Calle 30, no. 518, esq. 7, Miramar, Havana, tel: 7204 2516; https://travel.gc.ca/assistance/embassies-consulates/cuba. The Canadian embassy offers help to Australians in an emergency.

UK: Calle 34, no. 702, esq. 7, Miramar, Havana, tel: 7214 2200; www.gov.uk/world/organisations/british-embassy-havana.

US: Calzada e/ L y M, Vedado, Havana, tel: 7839 4100; https://cu.usembassy.gov/.

EMERGENCIES (see also Health and medical care and Police)

Asistur, a state-run organization, helps foreigners with medical or financial problems and is affiliated with a number of international travel insurance companies. If you are insured with them for a 10 percent commission, they can negotiate a cash advance if provided with bank details overseas. Asistur's main office is at Paseo del Prado, 208 e/ Colón y Trocadero, Old Havana, tel: 7866 4499, www.asistur.cu. There are also offices in Ciego de Avila, Holguín, Santiago and Matanzas.

Useful telephone numbers: Police 106, Fire 105, Ambulance 104, Information 113. These numbers may not work in remote areas so ask your hotel or *casa particular*.

G

GETTING THERE (see also Airports)

Most flights into Cuba arrive at Havana, Varadero and several other airports convenient to beach resorts such as Cayo Coco, Cayo Santa María and Guardalavaca. From Canada, scheduled flights to Cuba leave from Montreal or Toronto. There are also charters from Vancouver, Halifax and Ottawa. From Europe, Air France flies to Havana from Paris; Iberia and Air Europa fly from Madrid. Condor flies from Frankfurt. Charters also fly from Switzerland, Spain and Italy. New charter flights are due to launch from Manchester to Holguín and LGW to Cayo Coco in May 2024. From Australia and New Zealand, the options include travelling through Canada, Mexico or other points in Latin America.

Scheduled flights are now operating (in addition to charters) from the US to Cuba. American Airlines, Jet Blue, Delta, and United Airlines are the main carriers.

GUIDES AND TOURS

Many come to Cuba on package tours, which may include a group excursion or two. If you wish to travel independently and have found a hotel-airfare package that is cheaper than separate arrangements or airfare alone, you are not obligated to go along with the group once in Cuba. Plenty of people check into their resort hotels and take off on their own.

The most popular and straightforward way of exploring Cuba is on group excursions. However, these trips – available in any tourist hotel and led by English-speaking tour guides – may insulate you from the most interesting aspects of Cuban life. You can reach virtually the whole island from any resort on excursions; most are flexible and will allow you to break up a daytrip and stay overnight if you wish to explore on your own.

US citizens who visit Cuba from the US must comply with US government rules on travel to the island as defined by the Office of Foreign Assets Control (OFAC) i.e. straightforward tourism is not allowed. The easiest way for US citizens to visit the island independently is by fulfilling the "Support for the

Cuban People" category of travel. The "People-to-people" travel category was re-instated in 2022 but is only available for tour groups and not individual travellers (https://ofac.treasury.gov/faqs/topic/1541). Note that US citizens are prohibited from staying in or purchasing from multiple state-owned hotels and companies (www.state.gov/cuba-sanctions/cuba-restricted-list).

Note that these rules on travel to Cuba apply to any nationality that departs US soil for Cuba, not just US citizens.

Freelance "guides", offering to take you to *casas particulares* and *paladares* (privately run lodgings and restaurants) or obtain cigars and prostitutes, are omnipresent in Cuba. A new wave of private guides operating in the country offer everything from cooking classes to bike tours to music events.

H

HEALTH AND MEDICAL CARE (see also Emergencies)

Cuba has an excellent national health system plagued by shortages. There are no mandatory vaccinations required for travel to Cuba; nonetheless, some health professionals recommend vaccinations against typhoid and hepatitis A.

Although Cuban water is chlorinated, tap water is not generally safe to drink. Bottled mineral water *(agua mineral)* is available but not always so. Bring a water bottle with a filter. The most likely source of food poisoning is from unhygienic hotel buffet food. Cuban food is plain, and upset stomachs are less common than in many other countries.

The Cuban sun can burn fair-skinned people within minutes. Use plenty of sunscreen and wear a hat. It's also easy to become dehydrated, so be sure to drink plenty of water. Mosquitoes and sandflies are a menace from dusk to dawn in coastal resorts. Air conditioning helps keep them at bay, but apply insect repellent.

If you need to see a doctor, contact your hotel's reception desk. Large resort hotels have their own doctor. All the island's main resorts have an international clinic *(clínica internacional)*, as do Havana, Santiago de Cuba, Cienfuegos and Trinidad. Treatment is expensive, so proper insurance is essential; it is mandatory to have health insurance before you arrive in Cuba.

Every town has an all-night pharmacy (*farmacia*). The range of medicines has become severely limited. Resorts have better-stocked international pharmacies, though prices can be astronomical.

I'm sick. **Estoy enfermo(a).**
Where's the nearest hospital? **¿Dónde está el hospital más cercano?**
Call a doctor/dentist. **Llame a un médico/dentista.**

HITCH-HIKING

Hitching a ride in Cuba is easy and generally safe. If you do *hacer botella*, offer money to the driver who may or may not accept. If you're looking to hitch, the biggest problem you'll encounter is the paucity of vehicles (at least outside the major cities). Official hitchhiking stops with an *Amarillo* (a person dressed in yellow) coordinating state-owned vehicles to transport passengers out of town are found on the outskirts of towns and cities. If you are in a hire car and feel comfortable stopping for passengers, they will be very grateful.

L

LANGUAGE

The official language is Spanish. Increasing numbers of Cubans are learning English (French, Italian and other languages), and many people in the tourist industry are fluent, but you will most likely need some Spanish, especially outside tourist hotels and major resorts.

LGBTQ+ TRAVELLERS

The hardline Cuban policy on homosexuality has lessened in recent years (sex between consenting adults was legalized in 1979), and same-sex marriage was legalized in 2023. It is still not the most LGBTQ+-friendly place to visit, although there are a growing number of LGBTQ+ scenes in Havana and Santa Clara. A Pride parade to coincide with the International Day against Homophobia, Biphobia and Transphobia is held every year in Havana in May.

M

MAPS

The best road map of Cuba is "Guía de Carreteras" by the Directorio Turístico de Cuba but to be honest it's best to have maps downloaded onto your cell phone. Maps.me and Guru Maps are the best sources. Both work for offline navigation.

MEDIA

You will not receive much outside news in Cuba via the TV, although many tourist hotels offer CNN. The main national newspaper, *Granma*, is the mouthpiece of the government. A weekly *Granma* international edition is published in English, French, Portuguese and German.

Cuban national television is broadcast on eight state-owned national channels. Tourist hotels all have satellite TV.

Just about everyone in Cuba has a radio, and loud music is a constant background sound wherever you go (whether from radio, or performances on the streets). There are seven state-owned national radio stations and each province has its own station as well. Radio Reloj (Clock Radio) gives round-the-clock news on AM to the background noise of a ticking clock. A good proportion of the population now gets news via cellphones. Data on cell phones was legalized in December 2018.

MONEY

Currency. The "tourist currency", the peso convertible (CUC) and the Cuban peso (CUP) were unified in 2021. Cuban pesos are used to pay restaurant and bar bills, street snacks, museum entrances, taxis, local buses, souvenirs, crafts and fruit and veg and foods in local markets and *agromercados*. For everything else – all government-owned hotel reservations, including those managed by foreign operators such as Melia, the nationwide tourist coach service, Víazul, food and goods from "MLC" (Moneda Libremente Convertible) aka dollar stores found in towns and stores in hotels, and hire cars and petrol, cards must be used: debit or credit cards (not connected to a US bank) or pre-paid Tarjeta Clásica (costing US$3) bought from exchange bureaux (CADECA) where you can upload your hard currency cash (USD/Euro/£/Swiss franc/yen/ Mexican peso) to the USD card (www.cubatravel.cu/en/blog/Post/85738/ Methods-of-payment-in-Cuba-How-can-I-pay-in-Cuba).

Currency exchange. At the time of writing, the official rate of exchange is 120 pesos to the USD (www.bc.gob.cu). Bring plenty of cash and make sure that the notes are clean and undamaged; any notes with writing on them or tears will be rejected. There are banks and *casas de cambio* (exchange houses, called a CADECA) where you can exchange your money. The CADECA rates at airports, ports and hotels are worse than that of CADECA in town centres. (Pay your taxi in USD or Euro and change your money in city CADECAs). Since currency unification, a thriving widespread black market has emerged. Rates can be seen here https://eltoque.com/tasas-de-cambio-de-moneda-en-cuba-hoy. When you come to pay a restaurant bill and you choose to pay in a foreign hard currency (which all *paladares* and other private entities accept) you must ask what (unofficial) rate of change they use as this will affect the change you receive in CUP.

Credit cards *(tarjetas de crédito)*. Outlets that accept credit cards (Access/ MasterCard, Visa and others), include tourist shops, supermarkets, upmarket state hotels and restaurants, airlines, petrol stations and car hire companies (see above). Nevertheless, nobody should rely solely on credit cards, as not everybody accepts them and, even if they do, telephone lines are sometimes out of action so payments cannot be processed. Cuba remains a largely cash *(divisa)* economy although this is changing rapidly. Be aware that getting change from big notes is often difficult.

ATMs. Cuba has a growing network of automatic teller machines in cities. Several banks (Banco Financiero is one) and CADECAs give over-the-counter cash advances on credit or debit cards on production of a passport, but charge high commission.

May I pay with a credit card? **¿Se puede pagar con tarjeta de crédito?**

How much is that? **¿Cuánto es?**

O

OPENING HOURS

Offices are usually open weekdays from 8.30am to 5pm, with a one-hour lunch break. Some are open on Saturday mornings, from 8am to noon or 1pm. Banks are typically open weekdays from 8.30am to 3pm.

Some museums open daily, but most close for one day (usually Monday) and also close on Sunday at noon or 1pm. Typical museum hours are 8am until 5pm (sometimes 4pm). Regardless of when you go, you'll find several closed for renovations; make inquiries before travelling a long way.

Restaurants do not typically stay open very late; most close their doors around 10pm or even earlier. The exception is *paladares*, which are usually open from noon to 11pm or midnight.

Farmers' markets open early, from around 7am or even earlier, and close when traders decide to leave – usually between 4 and 6pm. Hard currency retail stores (often referred to as MLC or dollar stores) are all over Cuba; most open Mon–Sat 10am–5pm but may stay open later. MLC supermarkets usually open Mon–Sat 9am–6pm and Sun 9am–1pm. Many of the bigger stores open 9am–9pm.

P

POLICE

Most police are helpful and friendly, even though they occasionally harass Cubans (or, more specifically, anyone of dark skin colour who might be assumed to be Cuban) accompanying foreigners. If you are robbed, make sure you get a police report (this can be a time-consuming affair).

POST OFFICES

You can buy stamps *(sellos)* at hotels, although this costs more than if you buy them at post offices. Some stamps are not sticky and you have to ask a post office or hotel desk for glue. Cuba's post system is unreliable and slow. Postcards *(tarjetas postales)* sent to Europe take from two weeks to a month or more to arrive.

Post offices are generally open weekdays 8am to 5pm and Saturday 9am to 3pm. You'll find post offices in every rural town; cities have several branches. In Havana, the best one to use is the one in the *Hotel Habana Libre* in el Ve-dado (Calles L and 23). More efficient mailing services are available through DHL Worldwide Express. It has an office in Havana (https://mydhl.express.dhl/cu/en/contact-us.html).

PUBLIC HOLIDAYS

The following days are public holidays in Cuba:
January 1–2 Anniversary of the Triumph of the Revolution: Liberation Day
Good Friday usually April, sometimes March
May 1 International Workers' Day (Labour Day)
July 25–27 National Rebellion Day (July 26)
October 10 Independence Day
December 25 Christmas Day
December 31 New Year's Eve

R

RELIGION

Roman Catholicism in Cuba is strongly intertwined with Afro-Cuban religions such as *Santería* (see page 33). Many aspects of these religious practices can be experienced by visitors. The government blunted the power and influence of the Catholic Church in the early 1960s, but mass is still said in churches throughout the island, and since the Pope's visits to Cuba in 1998, 2012 and 2015 there has been a resurgence of Catholic practice. Evangelical churches are on the rise.

T

TELEPHONES AND INTERNET

Cuba's country code is 53. To make an international call from Cuba dial 119, then the country code, the area code and the phone number. Dial 113 for the free domestic telephone enquiries service.

Top hotels have direct-dial facilities for all calls. Elsewhere you can make domestic calls on a direct line, but you will need to go through the hotel operator for international calls. International calls from Cuba cost CUP25/minute. As they do everywhere in the world, hotels charge a significant surcharge on calls.

Public phones which take coins (5 or 20 centavos or CUP1) are now rare; most have been converted to take pre-paid phone cards *(tarjeta propia)*. Local, regional and interregional calls cost from CUP0.40 to CUP1 a minute. The state telecommunications company is ETECSA, also known as Telepunto, which offers a full range of services.

Most tourists now obtain a Cubacel Sim card – via a temporary line or a least-hassle tourist line which is now indispensable especially as many Cubans now use Whatsapp. Tourist sims (CubacelTur, http://cubaceltur.com) are valid for thirty days and can be bought online and picked up on arrival in Cuba. If there is a problem picking up on arrival or the Cubacel booth is closed, head to the nearest ETECSA office to your accommodation. A basic package comes with 6GB of data, 100 call minutes and 100 SMS. Cards can be topped up – for data only. Many *casa particulares* also offer guests use of a Sim card during their stay. The cost of data packages in CUP is extremely reasonable but once you've moved on to another city you will be without cover, so a "tourist" Sim card is the best option. You can use your own unlocked phone in Cuba (where there is a signal) and ask office staff to configure your phone for use. All mobile numbers begin with "5" and have eight digits.

If all else fails and you can't use your phone for a Cuban Sim card, public Wi-fi spots are available around the country. Access is via a prepaid Nauta card bought at ETECSA offices. One hour costs CUP12.50 but cards are often scarce.

Before you get to Cuba download a VPN. You cannot access Airbnb, for example, without a VPN when in Cuba.

I'd like make a telephone call … **Quisiera hacer una llamada …**
to England/Canada/United States **a Inglaterra/Canadá/los Estados Unidos**
reverse-charge call **cobro revertido**
Can you get me this number in … ? **¿Puede comunicarme con este número en … ?**
phone card **tarjeta telefónica**
sim card **un chip telefónica**
coverage **cobertura**
signal **señal**

TIME ZONES

Cuba is five hours behind Greenwich Mean Time (GMT). It operates on Eastern Standard Time in winter and Daylight Saving Time (one hour later) from April to October.

San Francisco	**Cuba**	New York	London	Sydney
9am	**noon**	noon	5pm	2am

TIPPING

Waiters and bellboys should be tipped either in pesos or in hard currency. Ten percent is usual for restaurant staff. Many *paladares* now add a service charge so check the bill first. You should leave around US$1 a day for a hotel chambermaid.

TOILETS

It's often best to carry a roll of toilet paper with you at all times in Cuba, as many establishments do not provide their own. Those that do often demand a few cents for providing it – so it's worth carrying some small change. Public loos are extremely rare. Your best bet are hotels, large restaurants and museums.

TOURIST INFORMATION

Canada: 1200 Bay Street, Suite 305, Toronto, Ontario M5R 2A5, tel: (416) 362 0700; www.gocuba.ca.

UK: 167 High Holborn, London WC1V 6PA, tel: (020) 7240 6655; www.cubavisa.uk.

In Cuba itself, there is no centralized system providing tourism information, and reliable information is sometimes hard to come by. Instead, you must rely upon hotels and travel agencies, whose primary function is to sell excursion packages. In Cuba all hotels have a tourism desk *(buró de turismo)*.

Infotur is the only tourist information service, although other state tour operators will help but are effectively useless.

TRANSPORT

Taxis. Taxis Cuba (tel: 7873 5701/7646 8104) in Havana are found all over Havana. You can call them or pick them up from designated ranks (outside hotels, major museums, bus stations and airports). They are sometimes metered but it's best to negotiate a fare before getting in the vehicle. Private taxis (classic cars, yellow taxis, Ladas and others which are licensed carry a yellow and black sticker in their window) circulate as do dozens of unlicensed vehicles. The lumbering vintage American cars with or without taxi signs *(colectivos* or *máquinas or almendrones)* have fixed routes. Spanish speakers can ask locals how to navigate these fixed taxi routes. Fixed-route Ruteros (yellow minibuses) can be hailed along any of their routes in Havana. Fares are very cheap. Grancar (tel: 7873 1410) runs a fleet of restored classic American cars but you can also find privately run classic vehicles parked outside major hotels and in front of the *Hotel Inglaterra* and Parque Central in Havana. Pre-book with a company such as Nostalgicar (www.nostalgicarcuba.com). Mainly outside of Havana, you will find electric vehicles (wagons) with seats in the back converted into taxis for urban transport. Before you get to Cuba download La Nave, Cuba's Uber, for door-to-door taxi rides.

Coco taxis. Havana's *cocotaxis* are yellow three-wheeled buggies powered by motorcycle engines. They are not particularly safe to travel in and fares are always inflated.

Bicycle taxis (*bicitaxis* or pedicabs). *Bicitaxis* are a fun way to traverse the city on short trips. The majority are found in Old Havana.

Buses (*guaguas*, pronounced "gwah-gwah"). Buses are the backbone of Cuba's public transport system, but urban buses in Havana are not a great option for tourists. There are too few of them, they're uncomfortable, they're usually full when they do arrive, there are long queues and there is a risk of being pickpocketed. A better option for tourists is the hop-on, hop-off service called the HabanaBusTour (www.rentcarcuba.com/en/pages/ver/bustour), with two routes, one from the Almacenes San José on Av del Puerto to Vedado, Plaza de la Revolución and Miramar (US$10) and the other from the Parque Central out to Playas del Este via the Castillo del Morro (US$5). A similar service runs from Varadero to Matanzas; from Trinidad to Playa Ancón; and around Viñales, the Bay of Pigs, Jardines del Rey, Guardalavaca, Holguín and Baracoa.

For travel between cities, towns and resorts of major tourist interest, however, use Víazul (Terminal de Omnibus, Av Independencia 101 esq. 19 de Mayo, Plaza de la Revolución, el Vedado; tel: 5989 0616; https://viazul. wetransp.com). It operates air-conditioned tour buses to Varadero, Viñales, Pinar del Río, Bay of Pigs, Cienfuegos, Trinidad, Santa Clara, Cayo Santa María, Sancti Spíritus, Ciego de Ávila, Jardines del Rey, Camagüey, Holguín, Las Tunas, Bayamo and Santiago de Cuba. Not all routes are running post-Covid so do check online first. Prices range from US$10 one way (Havana to Las Terrazas) to US$70 (Havana to Baracoa). It runs on time, seats are allocated, and tickets must be bought online. However, if seats remain for a particular journey, tickets can be bought two hours before departure at each Víazul office in bus terminals with a bank card. Children 11 and under travel at a discount with their own seat. Children aged under four who share a seat travel for free. Cubatur with Transtur also offers "The Cuba Express" bus service from Havana to Cienfuegos and Trinidad. Longer distance transfers have been known to run to Santiago. You can enquire and book at Cubatur desks in hotels. The bus service to Batabanó on the south coast to connect with the ferry service to the Isle of Youth leaves from the former Víazul bus station at Avenida Zoológico y 26 (tel: 7881 1413) now by the Viajeros Company (tel: 7698 7007/7698 7058). Foreigners can buy tickets from any Viajeros Agency office (tel: 7877 5644-46) around the country. Ferry tickets are CUP200 and the bus ticket is CUP10.

Trains (trenes). Train journeys are extremely slow, the schedules are unreliable and breakdowns are frequent. There are no express trains, almost all are local services. Trains run from Habana to Santiago, to Guantánamo, to Holguín and to Manzanillo every four days in rotation. The train between Havana and Santiago de Cuba takes at least fifteen hours, usually many more., so be prepared for a long journey. Habana-Santiago first class (in new Chinese carriages) is CUP122 and economic class is CUP95. Unfortunately at the moment, visitors can't reserve in advance but must go to the Estación Central (Arsenal y Ejido, La Habana Vieja) to enquire for last-minute tickets. For information: tel: 7862 1920.

Domestic flights. Flying in Cuba is not recommended. Cubana, the national airline, provides domestic flights to various destinations from the capital. Frequency varies enormously. Tickets can be purchased in Cubana offices around the country or from the main office in Havana on Calle 23 (La Rampa), no. 64 esq. Infanta (tel: 7834 1039), or at the airport, Terminal 3 (tel: 7649 0410). Cubana flying from Madrid stops in Santiago de Cuba en route to its final destination in Havana and stops again in Santiago on its way from Havana to Madrid.

Horse carts (coches). In virtually every city except Havana and Santiago there are horses pulling covered carts up and down the main streets. Ironically, horse carriages acting as taxis have become a tourist attraction in the resorts.

When's the next bus/train to…? **¿Cuándo sale el próximo guagua/tren para…?**
What's the fare to…? **¿Cuánto es la tarifa a…?**
A ticket to… **Un billete para…**
single (one-way) **ida**
return (roundtrip) **ida y vuelta**

V

VISAS AND ENTRY REQUIREMENTS

All visitors entering Cuba must show a passport valid for at least six months beyond the date of arrival in Cuba. Prior to arrival, visitors must fill out the online form D'Viajeros (www.dviajeros.mitrans.gob.cu/datosMigratorios) up to 48 hours before departure and present the QR code or print the form with the QR code (www.dviajeros.mitrans.gob.cu/assets/pdf/BeneficiosDViajeros.pdf). In addition, visitors must have a green tourist card (Tarjeta del Turista), issued by the Cuban Consulate directly or, more commonly, through a travel agent. This will be valid for thirty days, but can be extended. Immigration officials no longer stamp your passport. Do not lose the tourist card – you must show it when you leave the country. NB. If you've visited Cuba since January 12, 2021 and wish to travel to the US on its visa waiver scheme (ESTA) you will no longer be allowed to do so. (https://esta.cbp.dhs.gov) – on this date President Trump named Cuba a State Sponsor of Terrorism. You can still travel to the US but must apply for a B-2 visitor visa.

Travel for US citizens. Travel to Cuba for tourist activities remains prohibited by the US state; however travel under a general license for twelve categories for travel is permitted. This is not as complicated as it sounds for group travel (People to People category) and for individual travel (Support for the Cuban People category). For details, visit https://ofac.treasury.gov/faqs/topic/1541. Visitors who depart US soil for Cuba (including foreign nationals) must buy a more expensive pink Tarjeta del Turista available from airlines.

W

WEBSITES

From sites about the US embargo and travel restrictions to traveller recommendations, there is a wealth of information. A few sites worth exploring include the following:

www.dtcuba.com Cuban Tourist Directory site

www.cubatravel.cu Official tourist site

https://oncubanews.com/en/cuba/ English/Spanish website packed with latest news

www.cuba-junky.com A comprehensive site for all Cuba lovers.

www.gov.uk/foreign-travel-advice/cuba FCDO travel advice

WHERE TO STAY

The best hotels are joint ventures with private firms from Spain, Canada and other countries that manage the hotels. These are of an international standard. Many others, though, are a notch or two down from what you'd expect in Europe, North America or Asia. In Old Havana, hotels in renovated colonial mansions are run by Habaguanex (www.gaviotahotels.com/en/habaguanex-hotels) and are beautiful places to stay although not always up to scratch. At the inexpensive level, hotels around the island are often lacking in ambience and amenities.

Casas particulares – accommodation in private homes – are not only a better-quality and much cheaper alternative to the inexpensive hotels; they allow you a glimpse into unguarded Cuban life. Many private accommodations are also now independent apartments and boutique hotels. The latter are primarily found in Havana. Most private accommodation is now found on Airbnb. They generally cost US$20–150 per room, depending on the standard, location and the season. You'll find a very abbreviated list of recommended private-home *casas* following the regular hotel listings below; however, others are very easy to find.

The price categories below, in US dollars, are for a standard double room, excluding meals, in high season (mid-December to mid-April, July to August). Prices vary during other months. All hotels accept credit cards.

$$$$	over $150
$$$	$100–150
$$	$50–100
$	under $50

HAVANA

Old Havana

Mystique Habana $$$ *Prado esq. Colón, La Habana Vieja,* www.mystique resorts.com/resorts/habana. A newly opened medium-sized hotel that has been elegantly furnished in early 1900s décor. Breakfast and dining are on the rooftop terrace. This hotel is in an excellent location close to the Fine Arts and Revolution museums (see page 37).

Royalton Habana $$$$ *Prado esq. Malecón, La Habana Vieja,* www.royalton resorts.com/resorts/habana. A new hotel with a rooftop infinity pool overlooking the ocean and the ocean road, the Malecón. Luxury rooms have been decorated with a nod to Cuba's music and dance scene.

Hotel Sevilla Habana $$$ *Trocadero, 55 e/ Prado y Zulueta, La Habana Vieja,* www.hotelsevillahabana.com. This restored turn-of-the-twentieth-century establishment of Spanish and Moroccan inspiration has a sumptuous lobby, magnificent rooftop restaurant and excellent dining options. Guests have included Al Capone, Josephine Baker and Enrico Caruso, and scenes from Graham Greene's *Our Man in Havana* were set here. Revamped rooms are comfortable and stylish. Good pool, and incredible rooftop dining room.

El Vedado

Hotel Nacional de Cuba $$$$ *Calle O esq. 21, el Vedado,* www.hotelnacional decuba.com. A classic feature of Havana, this landmark 1930 hotel rises above the Malecón. Former guests include Hemingway, Churchill, Frank Sinatra, Ava Gardner, Errol Flynn, Marlon Brando and gangsters Meyer Lansky and Lucky Luciano. Rooms are large, and most have sea views. It has a stunning dining room, two pools, a nightly cabaret show, gardens, terraces and bars.

Meliá Cohiba $$$$ *Paseo e/ 1ra y 3ra,* www.melia.com/en/hotels/cuba/ havana/melia-cohiba. A modern hotel with plenty of facilities close to the ocean and Malecón which provides very good service and a lovely ground floor pool.

PINAR DEL RÍO AND ARTEMISA PROVINCE

Hotel E Central Viñales $$ *Calle Salvador Cisneros, Viñales,* https://e-central. hoteles-en-islas-del-caribe.com. This petite hotel with 23 rooms in the heart of Viñales village is in an excellent location and with great people watching opportunities with its tables on the front terrace and rooms with balconies overlooking main street.

Hotel Moka $$ *Las Terrazas, Artemisa,* www.lasterrazas.cu/en/hotel/hotel-moka. A welcoming hotel at the heart of the eco-community of Las Terrazas. Rooms across two floors feature bathtubs with floor to ceiling windows overlooking the teak tree forest and homes of the village. Life revolves around the bar and the restaurant, often brightened by a live band. Villagers staff the hotel.

Cayo Largo del Sur

Sanctuary at Grand Memories Cayo Largo $$$$ *Cayo Largo del Sur, tel: 4624 8079,* www.memoriesresorts.com/resorts/grand-cayo-largo. All the hotels on Cayo Largo del Sur are all-inclusive and managed by Canada's Blue Diamond. This low-key adults-only resort is made up of 45 wooden bungalows scattered throughout the tropical-planted gardens facing Playa Blanca.

MATANZAS PROVINCE
Varadero

Meliá Las Américas $$$$ *Playa Las Américas, Km 9, tel: 4566 7600,* www.meliacuba.com. This five-star hotel is a highly-ranked all-inclusive golf and beach resort offering international quality and facilities next to a lovely curve of beach which stretches towards the handsome *Mansión Xanadú*.

Meliá Varadero $$$$ *Autopista del Sur, Km 9, tel: 4566 7013,* www.meliacuba.com. Located next to the Plaza Las Américas Convention Center and Shopping Center, and the Varadero Golf Club. This is an all-inclusive megacomplex with tons of amenities: fountain, pool, restaurants, nightclub, shops and more.

Starfish Cuatro Palmas Varadero $$$$ *Avenida 1ra e/ 60 y 64, tel: 4562 3507,* www.starfishresorts.com. A low-key beachside complex with colonial-style villas and bungalows on either side of the road. Some of the rooms are arranged around an excellent pool. Convenient for downtown, nightlife and restaurants.

Zapata Peninsula

Villa Guamá $ *Laguna del Tesoro, Ciénaga de Zapata, tel: 4591 5551,* www.hotelescubanacan.com. Reached by boat, this is one of the most distinctive places to stay in Cuba, set out as a replica Taíno village. Thatched huts are spread over interconnected islands in the middle of a swamp. Mosquito repellent essential. Good for birdwatching. Crocodile on the menu. Temporarily closed for repairs at the time of writing.

CENTRAL CUBA

Cayo Coco

Tryp Cayo Coco $$$ *Cayo Coco,* www.meliacuba.com. One of Cuba's most attractive resort hotels, a replica of a colonial village amid palm gardens and a lagoon set in front of a dazzling white beach. The villas are interwoven by a magnificent sculpted pool. Watersports, diving centre, restaurants and shops are all available.

Cayo Guillermo

Iberostar Daiquirí $$$ *Cayo Guillermo,* www.ibercuba.com. A good, popular, all-inclusive family hotel, with bright, recently refurbished rooms, each with its own balcony. The hotel is set on a long, narrow beach with shallow sea. Good food, buffet or themed restaurants, nice pool, excellent service.

Camagüey

E Camino de Hierro $$ *Plaza de la Solidaridad, tel: 3228 4264,* www.cubanacahoteles.com. This colonial building in the heart of town has been renovated and is a small intimate hotel in the heart of the city. Rooms come with balconies and there are tables outside for coffee, beers and people watching.

Cienfuegos

La Unión $$$ *Ave 31 esq. 54,* www.meliacuba.com/en/destinationen/cienfuegos/hotels/la-union. The building dates from 1869 and has been restored making this one of the nicest places to stay in the area, but its town centre location means it can be noisy. Facilities include a business centre, gym, courtyard, pool (which can get very crowded), car rental, restaurant and bars.

Playa Santa Lucía

Brisas Santa Lucía $$ *Playa Santa Lucía,* www.cubanacanhoteles.com. A stalwart of the Camagüey coast, *Brisas Santa Lucía* is a low-key hotel with a strong programme of family activities.

Trinidad

Iberostar Grand Trinidad $$$$ *José Martí 262 y Lino Pérez,* www.ibercuba.com. This is the best centrally located hotel. Good service, good food in colonial style building. Expansion underway next door which will feature a swimming pool.

EL ORIENTE

Baracoa

Hotel El Castillo $$ *Calixto García, Loma del Paraíso, tel: 2164 5165.* One of Cuba's most charming hotels, converted from one of Baracoa's old forts. Perched on a cliff, it has a fine pool, gardens, mountain views, helpful staff and spacious bedrooms. A real bargain. Temporarily closed for repairs at the time of writing.

Villa Maguana $$ *Carretera a Moa Km 22, Playa Maguana, tel: 2164 1204.* A small hotel of two-storey cabañas set in gardens right next to beautiful Maguana Beach. It's low-key with limited food options but a lovely escape.

Guardalavaca

Paradisus Río de Oro Resort and Spa $$$$ *Playa Esmeralda,* www.meliacuba.com. This all-inclusive resort is the best in the area and one of the top hotels in Cuba, situated in its own pretty bay giving it an exclusive feel. Four very good restaurants including Japanese and Creole.

Santiago de Cuba

Hotel Casa Granda $$ *Heredia 201 esq. Parque Céspedes, tel: 2265 3021*, www.cubanacanhoteles.com. A grand white building in the heart of Santiago, overlooking the main plaza, this classic hotel is a great place for people-watching, but the rooms are nothing special. In its heyday Joe Louis and Graham Greene's "Man in Havana" stayed here. Terrace bar with amazing views.

Meliá Santiago de Cuba $$ *Av. de las Américas y Calle M*, www.meliacuba.com. Santiago's most ostentatious hotel, 3km (2 miles) from the centre with lots of facilities including a luxury pool.

CASAS PARTICULARES (PRIVATE LODGINGS)

Baracoa

Villa Paradiso Baracoa $ *Moncada 92-B,* https://villaparadisobaracoa.com. A super lovely casa with a couple of rooms, fabulous balcony and very attentive hosts who can arrange tours. Great food available.

Havana

Baywinds $ *Aguiar St no.114 apt 701 e/ Chacón y Cuarteles, Old Havana, tel: 5245 1310,* amaurypbello@gmail.com. An independent apartment with terraces decorated with contemporary art, at the heart of the bars and restaurants of trendy northern Old Havana. Amaury, the owner, has a more moderately priced self-contained one-bed apartment, *El Nido*, in the same building, too.

Casa Vitrales $$$ *Habana 106 e/ Cuarteles y Chacón, Old Havana,* https://cvitrales.com. A beautifully restored early twentieth-century building with nine rooms all gorgeously designed marrying antique pieces with modern accessories. A rooftop terrace with winning views is where breakfast is served. It's right in the heart of trendy northern Old Havana.

Melba and Alberto $ *Galiano 115, Apt 81, e/ Animas y Trocadero, Centro, tel: 7863 5178/5264 8262,* barracuda1752@yahoo.es. Rooms in an apartment on the eighth floor with great views from the balconies and worlds away from the down-at-heel street life of Centro. Comfortable rooms with use of kitchenette.

Santa Clara

Casa Mercy $ *San Cristóbal 4 e/ Cuba y Colón, tel: 4221 6941,* casamercy@gmail.com. *Casa Mercy*'s charming hosts offer two spacious rooms overlooking the street in this comfortable house which is very central. There is also a pleasant roof terrace for cocktails. Excellent food offered and any diet accommodated.

Santiago de Cuba

Casa Dulce $ *San Basilio, 552, esq. Clarín, tel: 2262 5479,* gdcastillo20@yahoo.es. Apartment upstairs on the corner, with large windows to catch the breeze. Comfortable room, charming English-speaking hostess, and a pleasant roof terrace with spectacular views of the city.

Hostal Girasol $ *Calle Santa Rita 409 e/ Carnicería y Calvario, tel: 2262 0513,* hostalgirasol1983@gmail.com. This is a great place to stay and to meet other travellers as the owners have several rooms and a terrace. A happy, sunny casa just a few minutes' walk from downtown.

Roy's Terrace Inn $ *Santa Rita 177, tel: 2262 0522,* roysterraceinn@gmail.com. A smart casa close to the Padre Pico steps, also a great spot to meet other travellers. There are rooms across several levels and a rooftop terrace restaurant serving delicious food.

Trinidad

Casa Colonial Muñoz $ *José Martí 401, e/ Fidel Claro y Santiago Escobar, tel: 4199 3031,* https://casa.trinidadphoto.com. Colonial house built in 1800 with a shady patio and roof terrace, and large rooms furnished with antiques. One of the finest *casas* in Cuba. Horse riding can be arranged.

Casa Font $ *Gustavo Izuierdo 105, e/ Piro Guinart y Simón Bolívar, tel: 5359 2740*, viatrifont@yahoo.es. Leo and Beatriz are a lovely family renting a room in a handsome eighteenth-century mansion in the heart of the town. The house has a nice patio, too, for alfresco breakfasts.

Hostal el Oasisabel $ *Frank Pais 389 e/ Desengaño y Rosario, tel: 5271 1776*, tereleria@gmail.com. A lovely home run by the friendly Teresa, the ultimate host, with a lush patio garden and several rooms. A few blocks from the central park in a quiet location.

Viñales

Casa Deborah y Juan Carlos $ *detrás del Policlínico, tel: 4879 6207*, deborah susana7@gmail.com. A family friendly home with two rooms around a central leafy patio situated just behind the main plaza. Super comfortable and very central.

INDEX

THE **MINI** ROUGH GUIDE TO
CUBA

First edition 2024

Editor: Libby Davies
Author: Claire Boobbyer
Picture Editor: Tom Smyth
Cartography Update: Carte
Layout: Greg Madejak
Head of DTP and Pre-Press: Rebeka Davies
Head of Publishing: Sarah Clark
Photography Credits: 123RF 80, 89;
Dreamstime 5M, 5T, 16, 91, 96; iStock 1, 4ML,
4ML, 7T, 7B, 21, 52, 67; Mockford & Bonetti/Apa
Publications 19; Shutterstock 4TL, 5T, 5T, 5M,
5M, 6T, 6B, 36, 58, 60, 79, 101, 102, 103; Sylvaine
Poitau/Apa Publications 5M, 11, 12, 14, 24, 26, 29,
31, 32, 35, 39, 40, 41, 43, 44, 47, 49, 51, 53, 55, 57,
63, 64, 69, 70, 73, 75, 76, 78, 83, 84, 86, 93, 94, 104
Cover Credits: Palacio de Valle in Cienfuegos
Rostislav Ageev/Shutterstock

Distribution
UK, Ireland and Europe: Apa Publications (UK)
Ltd; sales@roughguides.com
United States and Canada: Ingram Publisher
Services; ips@ingramcontent.com
Australia and New Zealand: Booktopia;
retailer@booktopia.com.au
Worldwide: Apa Publications (UK) Ltd;
sales@roughguides.com

**Special Sales, Content Licensing
and CoPublishing**
Rough Guides can be purchased in bulk
quantities at discounted prices. We can create
special editions, personalised jackets and
corporate imprints tailored to your needs.
sales@roughguides.com; http://roughguides.com

Printed in Czech Republic

This book was produced using **Typefi** automated
publishing software.

Contact us
Every effort has been made to provide accurate
information in this publication, but changes
are inevitable. The publisher cannot be held
responsible for any resulting loss, inconvenience
or injury sustained by any traveller as a result
of information or advice contained in the
guide. We would appreciate it if readers would
call our attention to any errors or outdated
information, or if you feel we've left something
out. Please send your comments with the
subject line "Rough Guide Mini Cuba Update" to
mail@uk.roughguides.com.